Also by Julie Mars

The Secret Keepers

Praise for *The Secret Keepers*

"Atmospheric, taut, and psychologically rich...an unusually smart debut."
—*Publishers Weekly*

"As spellbinding and entertaining as it is (not allowing the reader to take a break before finally finishing it off in one sitting), *The Secret Keepers* is also a familial/morality based tale with its heart poignantly set on the likelihood that we live in a world of redemption."   —*The Daily Yomiuri*

"The level of tension Mars maintains keeps the story suspenseful and entertaining...an all-around, satisfying read."   —*PIF Magazine*

"A spectacular story...a wonderful tale, drawing readers in from the beginning and leaving them wanting more."   —*Virginia Quarterly Review*

"Mars writes in a crisp fast pace with many plot twists and turns. The characters come to life with gritty humanity."   —*Albuquerque Journal*

"Mars' prose is sharp as a razor, her observations dead on. An intelligent thriller for intelligent readers."   —*Oregon Statesman Journal*

"An impressive debut novel... The plot is fast-paced, with plenty of twists and turns...The story is character driven. The pleasure comes in learning who the people are, and watching them grow beyond what they were when we first met them."   —*Waycross Journal-Herald*

"An involving read, just what you need for those chilly, spooky jack o'lantern nights."   —*MyPrimeTime.com*

"Mars weaves a clever web."   —*The Anniston Star*

"*The Secret Keepers* is a book you just can't put down. Mars is moving away from thrillers where evil characters appear and involve the normal protagonists in intrigue. Her genre alteration would mean she is identifying a new tension in our society… She begins by following all the rules of the thriller and then rudely sets aside the genre's prime directive by making the innocent bystanders the actual perpetrators of the crime."
—*American Book Review*

"This excellent first novel fooled me at first… As I got into [it] I couldn't put it down."   —*Easton Star Democrat*

"[The characters] are delightfully human, original, and likely to stay with the reader long after the last page is devoured."   —*Miami Today*

"*The Secret Keepers* will be one of the year's best books… Seek it out, if not for its literary merit, then for its powerful message of redemption."
—*Ron Chapman, KUNM – NPR*

"This debut novel starts out calmly enough, as if the author is driving a taxi slowly down a New York street, pointing out quirky neighborhood characters. Then, when the introductions are over, she puts the pedal to the metal, there's a rush of acceleration and the ride gets fast and wild. The pages seem to turn of their own volition."   —*Foreword Magazine*

"*The Secret Keepers* will leave you wanting more, desperate to continue a journey that leaves you looking for those last few explanations."
—*Single Mom Magazine*

"Edgy, dark and intelligent…the action escalates, the tension holds, …there may be an epiphany…and joy…at the end of the long and breath-holding chase that ends this fine novel. Good going, Julie Mars."
—*Taconic Newspapers*

"Mars has a delightful way to stimulate your gray cells."
—*New Jersey Current*

"I gobbled up this book, and when it ended I wanted to begin at the beginning again for the sheer pleasure of its breathtaking language and imagery. Mars is a major new talent."   —*The River Reporter*

A Month of Sundays

Searching
for the Spirit
and My Sister

A Month of Sundays

Searching
for the Spirit
and My Sister

JULIE MARS

GREYCORE PRESS

In instances where the identity of individuals was of concern, I have used pseudonyms to protect the privacy of the individuals in question.

Cover and text design by Kathleen Massaro

GREYCORE PRESS
www.greycore.com

Mars, Julie.
        A month of Sundays : searching for the spirit and my sister / by Julie Mars.
        p. cm.
        Includes index.
        LCCN 2004116731
        ISBN 0-9742074-5-4
        ISBN 0-9742074-6-2

        1. Mars, Julie. 2. Mars, Julie—Family relationships. 3. Spiritual biography. 4. Death— Religious aspects. 5. Brothers and sisters—Death—Psychological aspects. 6. Bereavement—Religious aspects. 7. Carter, Shirley (Shirley Ann)—Death and burial. 8. Religious institutions. 9.Self-actualization (Psychology) I. Title.

        BL73.M377A3 2005   204'.4'092
                                        QBI04-800135

This book is dedicated, with love and gratitude,
to Marcia Hennessy,
Joan and Jerrie Hutchison,
and Wies Van Lier.

Acknowledgements

I wish to thank Joan Schweighardt. Without Joan, nothing.

For her encouragement, steadfast belief in this book, and wise and patient help, draft after draft, I thank Theresa Park.

For their help and support while I took care of Shirley, grieved for her, or wrote this book, I want to thank Marietta Benevento, the Carter Clan, Janet D'Arcangelo, Robert Farris, Minrose Gwin, the wonderful people at Hospice of the North Country, Jennifer Hix, Mary Lou Kingsley, Michele Meyers, Laura and John Murphy, Chris Newbill, Kenshin Nishikubo, Julie Reichert, Paul Rymniak, Julie Shigekuni, Mary Anne Staniscewski, Mary Starling, Alexcia Trujillo, Judith Van Gieson, Sharon Oard Warner, and Whitney Woodward.

Table of Sundays

Preface

For seven months, I took care of my sister, Shirley, who was dying of pancreatic cancer. When she received her diagnosis in June 2000, I rushed there, to her little farmhouse at the end of a dirt road in upstate New York not far from the border of Canada. My motivation was complex. First, I loved her. I felt I owed her my life because, true or not, when I was a child I felt certain in my heart that she was the only one in the whole wide world who loved me. I wanted to be there for her, as she had been there for me. But there was something more to it.

Maybe seven years ago, I had a dream in which I was playing poker with four other people. At that time, one of them, in real life, was desperately ill with ovarian cancer. She has since died. Another player had recently been diagnosed with breast cancer. Thankfully, she is alive and well. Though it was not diagnosed at the time, the third player died two years later of liver cancer. The fourth player I have lost touch with. I'm the fifth player in this card game.

I woke up from this dream seriously afraid. Life-and-death is high stakes poker, especially knowing that everyone ultimately loses. Now, years later, again and again, this dream comes back to me, vividly. I keep picturing the round oak table, perfect for playing poker, in Shirley's kitchen. In my mind, I see my sister there, alone.

So I go to Shirley. This involves dropping everything. The Ph.D. program I am two years into. My book tour, following the publication of my first novel, *The Secret Keepers*. My life in New Mexico. I feel no conflict about this. And I spend seven months with my sister, who is well along her personal path toward death. Like a shadow, her death is present in each bright moment, of which there are many, even up to her last breath. Because I truly believe she is heading into the heart of the mystery, I watch her carefully and listen to her with extreme attention. I witness her intense spiritual turbulence and her ultimate return to Catholicism as, physically immobilized, she tears at breakneck speed through a dark landscape of religious doubt toward her God. I consider it an honor and a privilege to be with her, every day, as she reflects on the state of her soul.

I do it, too, because it's catching.

Myself, I have never felt farther from Catholicism, though I was raised a Catholic, as Shirley was. Now, I listen to tapes on the Tibetan art of living and dying before I fall asleep at night. If I sleep. I do whatever my sister needs—make phone calls to priests, share her anxieties about making her first confession in three decades, plow up memories of why she left the Catholic church so long ago. When a nice nun gives her a mantra to repeat, I type it up and tape it to her bedside table. I buy her a tape of Paul Timmons reciting the rosary. He is a Catholic charismatic who has attempted to heal Shirley by faith. When he comes to a nearby town to conduct a spiritual event, I go and report back to Shirley, verbatim.

But I don't believe. As my sister's faith forms its final shape and hardens, mine disappears. And when Shirley dies, horribly, and gets to return, at last, to a Catholic church for her funeral mass, I leave that church disgusted because the priest has used her precious funeral to preach against abortion and living in sin. I want to get my sister's body out of there, away from bloody images of the crucified savior, away from the empty pomp and circumstance, away from that awful priest.

Still, when I return home, to Albuquerque, I feel a driving need of only two specific activities in my life. One is to see people dance. Fortunately, a series of dance performances is about to begin, and a pass to all six is only thirty dollars. When I arrive at the KiMo Theater box office, the season tickets aren't available yet, and the box office person (I don't know why) gives me free tickets to all the shows. Last night, I went to a performance in which dancers spiraled, leaped, spun, rolled, and catapulted themselves about the stage.

My second serious desire is to go to church.

I am surprised and a little afraid of this, so I set up some ground rules for myself. I will go to church every Sunday for thirty-one weeks: a month of Sundays. I will dress up and arrive a half hour early to take a picture with Shirley's simple camera, which I have taken from her farmhouse. I will enter the church five minutes early and sit somewhere in the middle.

I will open my heart to the spirit.

True Vine at Five Points Baptist Church
Albuquerque, NM

I feel giddy getting dressed, putting on my black tights and cleaning the mud off my winter boots. My friend Julie Reichert, the cancer survivor from my dream, has helped me load Shirley's camera and said I look nice in my church outfit. I have selected the True Vine Baptist Church for my first Sunday. It is the only church I have ever noticed in my neighborhood, perhaps because it's located a half mile from my house at a particularly busy intersection where five South Valley roads cross. There is usually a long line at the traffic light there, which permits me, rare in this western car culture, to take a moment to look around at my own neighborhood. I have periodically seen the True Viners standing together outside the church. Possibly, I have noticed them because most are black in a city where the African American population is only five percent. I have seen pressed white shirts and ties on the men, colorful dresses and even hats on the women, and once, when the door was open in the hot weather, I heard beautiful gospel music coming from inside. So I pick this church.

Honestly, I know nothing about the Baptist church, other than it's Christian, which in my current state of mind is not a point in its favor. I am still furious at Shirley's funeral priest. But I put all that aside, an anthropologist doing field work, and suddenly I remember that more than two decades ago, in college, I took a class in the anthropology of religion. Through all the intervening years, the definition of religion, as supplied to budding anthropologists by Clifford Geertz, emerges in my mind: religion is a system of beliefs that imbues everyday events with mystical overtones and treats this created world as if it is really real. I remember this definition precisely, as if I'd memorized it yesterday. I jot it down on a yellow legal pad, put the pad and Shirley's camera into my bag, and start my car feeling that I am heading into a big adventure, though I am only going four blocks.

It has snowed—rare in Albuquerque—and I drive carefully down Bridge Boulevard toward the Rio Grande, past the True Vine on my right. At the light at Five Points, I take a left and circle around through two parking lots and stop across Bridge, directly facing the church. I arrive at 10:20, and the place is deserted, which suits me fine, because I am self conscious as I climb from the car to take my True Vine photo. I have never had a camera and never take pictures. I am so nervous about having loaded this one incorrectly that I have brought along a throwaway for backup. I position myself on the median between the east and west-bound lanes of Bridge Boulevard and take a few shots.

I focus first on a big sign, posted on the side of the building: "Come worship with us—Everyone welcome!" Truthfully, I don't feel welcome in church. Church is for believers, I think, not for people like me who are so consumed with doubt, they don't believe in anything at all. Who are suspicious of faith and who don't trust the Christian right. Who seriously considered, with Shirley's best friend Marcia, a self-proclaimed sinner, whether the roof might blow off the Catholic church when we stepped over the threshold for Shirley's funeral.

I return to the car with cold, wet feet. The day I left Shirley's, the snow was two feet deep and the temperature was below zero. Here, I watch the icicles along the church roof melt. They drip so fast that the whole long row could pass for public art—a fountain designed especially for the True Vine Baptists. I wonder how this modest little church will look inside, what the topic of the sermon will be, if the churchgoers will welcome me, like the sign promises, or glance at me sideways, singling me out as an intruder. At least nobody saw me with the camera on the median strip. I feel safer knowing this.

At quarter to eleven, it's still completely, ridiculously quiet at the True Vine Baptist Church, and suddenly it hits me that maybe, despite the sign, there won't be a Sunday morning worship at eleven. Does this happen? Can it?

I feel sick just thinking of it. This is my first step. This is my first Sunday.

This is my search for the spirit.

If nobody shows up, does that mean the spirit has deserted this place—and me? That I, and all the people who used to gather here, have been flatly rejected—by God, no less? That I picked, of all the churches in Albuquerque, the one that has packed up and gone out of the spiritual business?

I look around the strip mall in whose parking lot I am waiting. Selene's Novedades, the Zapateria Pedrito, and the Imperial Furniture are all closed. Their doors are locked and barred. But that makes sense. It's Sunday. Shops are closed, and churches are open.

I watch two Hispanic kids in T-shirts and sunglasses throw snowballs at each other in their front yard.

Nobody comes to open the doors of the True Vine, and when it's just ten minutes to show time, I hear myself chuckling—a strange combination of amusement and dread, acceptance and resentment. If there is a God, I think, this God must like to sock it to people like me. In all good faith, I have come to church, and, as they say in the North Country where Shirley lived and died, By God, I'm gonna go.

I get out of the car and cross the street.

I know the door will be locked, and it is.

I feel completely lost as I jiggle the doorknob and cup my hands around my eyes to peer through the narrow windows. I see nothing. Then, still hoping, I cross the little church yard to the other building in the compound, and I try that door. It's locked, too.

But standing there, locked out and alone, I happen to notice a brass plaque set into the stucco at the corner of the building, and, with nothing better to do this Sunday morning, I wander over to read it. It says:

Organized August 7, 1987
Dr. L. E. Hightower, President

State Conference of New Mexico
Dr. V. L. Bobbs, Pastor
S. Bradford, Deacon
J.C. Carter, Deacon
W. Carter, Deacon
Pat Walts, Secretary/Treasurer
Dorothy Bobbs, Director of Missions
Anna Carter, Mother of Church
Donated by Crestview Funeral Home

Shirley's married name, her last name, was Carter.

Carter, says the sign. Carter, Carter, Carter. Shirley has two sons and a daughter with the first initial J and another son with the initial W. And her middle name was Ann.

Anna Carter, the sign says. Mother of Church.

It's worth a picture to me, and as I slide the protective door back from the camera lens, I suddenly remember an e-mail I received from Shirley's friend Marcia just three days ago:

> Peggy (the blonde who sat next to me in church and at Shirley's memorial and still works at the nursing home) just called me to tell me the following: there has been a man at the nursing home for years who has gigantism (—he's well over seven feet tall, probably more, and is a little slow which makes him very open and therefore uncomplicated). He is dying and has had a visit from Shirley! She adored him, and he, her. She took care of him all the years she worked there. He has told people that he has seen Shirley, that he is not afraid, and that he is "ready to go home." He has no agenda to make this up. It is my fervent belief that HE HAS SEEN SHIRLEY and that she will take him home to wherever she is. Sounds like something Shirley would do. She will lead the way for him. What do you think? Do pass this along to her kids if you think that is appropriate.

Immediately, I forwarded it to Shirley's kids. Then I called my and Shirley's mother. "Shirley has been spotted!" I said as soon as she picked up the phone.

"By who?" she asked, and when I told her it was Shirley's giant, she said, "Oh, yes!" We have all heard about him from Shirley, who worked as a nurse's aide in a county nursing home for twenty-two years.

I get her camera focused on the plaque as best I can.

Water drips fast from the icicles.

I cry every morning about Shirley, who died on Christmas night, just one month ago.

I look at the plaque, bright gold in the New Mexico sunlight.

Carter, Carter, Carter. Mother of Church.

Shirley Ann Carter, my sister, had a great sense of humor and loved to laugh. Her laughter and her smile were bright beyond belief. They had healing power. Did she send me here, I wonder, to this particular church in which, at least for this week, I won't be finding any spirit? I don't know. But maybe.

I cross the street and get back in my car.

Wednesday

Every morning I wake up around five, when it is dark and quiet. I light a candle. Irrationally, I feel I must do this so Shirley, who has never visited me in New Mexico—or anywhere else, for that matter—can find me. The candle came from the Sanctuario at Chimayo, one of the oldest Catholic churches in the United States. It is a place where, at least in legends, miracles happen. The dirt there is considered holy. In a small room next to the altar, a hole has been cut in the concrete floor and red dirt is visible. Pilgrims from everywhere are allowed to take a little. I have visited the Sanctuario three times since I've lived in New Mexico (I don't know why), and each time I take a handful of this dirt. One of them, I put in a plastic toothbrush box and gave to Shirley. I found that box under her pillow after the undertakers had come to take her body away for the last time, out of the house, the bedroom, the bed that had become her universe.

The rest of the dirt, I leave loose in the cup holder on the dashboard of my 1988 Dodge Colt Vista. My dashboard is currently covered with desert items: petrified wood, old stones, dried sticks. The Chimayo dirt blows around when the windows are open, leaving a film on everything. I don't care. It is holy dirt. All dirt is holy, I think. Besides, I have seen the woman who tends the church bring it in from outside by the bucketful and dump it into the hole in the floor, which takes some of the mystery out of it. It was she who gave my friend Madalyn three candles in red glasses when we visited the chapel on New Year's Day, 2000. Immediately, on the spot, Madalyn gave one to me. I never lit it until I began to light it every day, for Shirley.

I like to reflect on life (and death) as the morning light arrives. I like to think over important events as a way of cementing them in my memory. But this week, I am realizing how much of the past seven months with Shirley—but most particularly, the last two weeks of her life, when she took what I have come to call the Final Dive—is a blur. I want to remember what happened which day, who was there. I have made a calendar and stared at it, filling in the squares with small events, as if by putting pencil marks inside the borders of each day, I can tame the events themselves. I have called one of our sisters and four of Shirley's six children with the same question: Which days were you there? Can you remember, exactly, what Shirley said and did on those days?

I have, in my mind, divided the Final Dive into three stages. One: Shirley is totally bedridden, totally helpless, but mentally alert. Two: Shirley is speaking in English, but often incoherently. Ranting. Three: Shirley as we knew her is gone but her body is alive. The technical term for this, we learn from Hospice, is non-responsive. The coma state. I feel compelled to know exactly when each stage began and ended.

But nobody's memory is clear. We contradict one another. Sometimes we think things happened during the final two weeks that actually happened a month before. And sometimes the reverse. "When did you buy all the books of logic problems?" I ask my nephew Johnny. "It was on an earlier trip," he says. But it wasn't. He made eight trips to see his mother since the summer. Six hundred and fifty miles each time.

During the Final Dive, Shirley's kids—I say kids though they range in age from thirty-three to forty-two—did those logic problems, obsessively, while I stretched out on the couch and read *Mad* magazine, which was the most intellectually challenging reading I did for the final three months. I had been there a long time. Officially melted down. I lived on chocolate milkshakes, peanut M&Ms, and caffeine-free Diet Pepsi. I read *Mad* magazine, sometimes aloud, even if nobody listened.

Today, though, I am not there but home. I have my first acupuncture appointment since returning to Albuquerque. I feel, have felt, in desperate need of it but have had to wait until now, the end of the month, due to financial strain induced by seven months out of the work loop. I lived on credit cards and cash advances—something Shirley did not approve of. I kept it secret from her, mainly.

In the waiting room of Alexcia Trujillo's acupuncture office, I pick up a book called *The Amazing Brain* and turn to the chapter on memory. I have always had an excellent memory, but neither I nor anyone else who was there can remember Shirley's last two weeks—at least not moment by moment. I choose a random paragraph and begin to read:

> Memories are stored among the neurons of the brain in some kind of relatively permanent form as physical traces, which we call memory traces. If only we knew the code, we could read the entire lifetime of experiences and knowledge from these traces in the brain.

I lift my eyes from the book to stare at the pale yellow wall in wonder. My memory traces of Shirley, my whole life with her, are precious to me. I don't want to forget her nor replace a lifetime of memories with the strange, pre-death, two-week fog. Interestingly, paradoxically, nothing feels as threatened as the most recent time period, her last time period, though much of the problem is trying to fit what happened then into those little squares I have drawn on a legal pad—the ones marked December 11th, December 12th, December 13th, and so on. My niece, Shirley's older daughter, also named Julie (both of us for my mother), has said that we can't pin anything down because time had no relevance by then. I distinctly remember that altered space, altered state, altered time, when Julie and I would immediately write it down when we gave Shirley her various medications, because five minutes later neither of us could remember if we had done it. How we laughed over our medical record in which I had flipped the page labeled Thursday to start the next one and labeled it Tuesday. Time, those last two weeks, was like the sea, and we were floating in it, sinking through it, taking it into our lungs.

For months, each of us who loved Shirley had told her, directly, that we freed her to "go." Letting go, telling her that we released her to her own destiny, was horrible to the extreme, an act of selflessness which no one felt competent to make, but one by one, no matter how excruciating, we all did it because we couldn't bear to see her suffer any more. I was there when our mother, eighty-eight years old and losing her second born, called Shirley on the phone. I had visited my mother to tell her she must do this. "Shirley," my mother said, for she had rehearsed a speech which she performed for me afterward, "I love you with all my heart, and if there was any way that I could change places with you, I would. But I'm ready to let you go."

Shirley's death was like a booby prize that everyone was forced to unwrap in front of her. As she got worse, we said it over and over again. "You don't have to stay, Shirley." I had specific words ready—words from my Buddhist tapes: "We will never forget you. You will always be with us and we will always be with you. We love you, now and forever. But we let you go." I said these words until I was blue in the face, as my mother would say, starting in August when we thought she would die any day. Any minute. I said them clear-eyed and matter-of-factly because the Buddhist tapes say that caregivers should get their crying and grieving done early so later, when the dying person is weaker, they won't be so emotional. It's unfair to cry too much, the tapes say, at the end. It creates emotional turbulence for the dying person, who has to focus on her caregivers instead of herself.

But suddenly, several days before Shirley dies, when she is in Stage Three of the Final Dive, my niece has a stunning insight: We also have to give her our permission to take as long as she needs or wants to die. Now we troop back into her bedroom to whisper, "You can go or stay, Shirley. We are here for you, as long as you need us, no matter what. No matter how much time you need." We say this into her ear when there is no sign of Shirley anywhere, except her body which doesn't even look like her anymore. Red marks, a sign of liver failure, have spread across her chest until they meld into scarlet blotches, and her skin is a color I've never seen in nature. "That's the color I want to be for Halloween!" her grandson, Alan, had said when he saw her in October.

I remember how Shirley laughed.

When Alexcia is ready for me, during our pre-acupuncture treatment conference, words gush, spew, tumble out of my mouth. I wake up once or more every hour, I tell her, all night long. Once, recently, I sat up screaming, "I'm gonna die!" And after I composed myself by saying out loud, "It's O.K. Everybody dies," I looked at the clock and saw that I'd been asleep exactly twenty-eight minutes. I have no balance and am falling over in every pose during my Beginner's T'ai-chi class. I don't like to leave the house. I have heart palpitations. I itch. I can't concentrate. Ever since I've returned to Albuquerque, I have had a horrible metallic taste in my mouth, and it doesn't go away, no matter how many glasses of water I drink.

"In Chinese medicine, that's grief," Alexcia says. "The metallic taste comes from the lungs, which are in charge of the breath. The breath takes in and lets go." She pauses. "Taking in and letting go," she repeats.

Can I let go of grief without letting go of Shirley? I told Shirley over and over again that she could go. I watched her go, helped her go, listened as her daughter Julie talked her over the Great Divide. "Your body doesn't need to breathe any more, Mom. Your heart does not need to beat. Don't panic," Julie was saying, and I felt my own heart ache with love for her and Shirley.

I saw Shirley's last breath.

I was there when she let go.

We didn't touch her at the end. She had waited so long and tried so hard to die that we were instinctively afraid—Julie, Shirley's youngest son, Neal, and I, who were with her—that if we touched her she would feel summoned, compelled to come back into that ravaged body.

Can I keep her memory and let everything else go?

They hurt today, the needles. Little explosions inside my skin. Alexcia says my lung and liver meridians are blocked, shut down. The chi is not flowing. I have weak blood and a troubled mind. I lie there, staring at a mobile that tosses rainbows into the room, until I climb off the table an hour later.

I post-date a check, just for tomorrow, but Alexcia flatly refuses to take my money. "I care about you," she says.

I am pierced, freshly, by her generosity.

That night, I only wake up three times.

When I get up at five in the morning, this morning, there's just a little metal in my mouth.

The Baha'i Center
Albuquerque, NM

I have phoned ahead to the Baha'i Community Center of Albuquerque to make sure they're still in the church business because being locked out once was amusing to me, but enough. They have a lunch at noon and a service from one until two-thirty. I agonize over whether I have to go to the lunch. Shirley would not have gone. She disliked crowds and social gatherings. She didn't even like to leave her little house. We came there instead and found her happy.

I have chosen the Baha'i faith because many years ago, a student of mine, a young woman with wild, jet black hair and eyes bright with confidence, strongly advised me to give it a try. This was in L.A., though it could easily have been New York, the Catskills, the Adirondacks, or New Mexico. For the past thirteen years, I have been an itinerant teacher of freshman composition. Two years ago, I resigned from my Assistant Professorship at a community college in New York to return to graduate school. "Why?" my colleagues asked. "You already have the job that a Ph.D. would buy you." "I don't care a bit about the degree," I replied.

"It's the reading and writing life I crave." I picked up and left the east, drawn to the good life, the reading and writing life, in the desert. And it was good, very good. And then Shirley got sick, and it all ended.

I lift Shirley's camera off the table, and for no reason, peer through the viewfinder. I am looking at the wall, looking at nothing, remembering how Shirley hated to have her picture taken. After she received her final diagnosis, though, overnight, she allowed it every time because we all wanted a picture with her, individual and group shots. I remember how my sister learned to face the camera and smile. How she learned to pose.

A few days after she died, I was searching for a video I had made of our father on his ninetieth birthday. He had performed one of his many shticks over his birthday cake, and I captured it with a videocam borrowed from my job. Later, watching it, I felt a rare flood of affection for my father. "He's adorable," I said out loud, shocking myself. When I recounted this to Shirley, she pronounced the video a priceless treasure, and she offered to keep it safe for me forever. Immediately, she tucked it under the skirt of her Victorian living room table. When I looked there, though, I found not one but a whole stack of unlabeled videos. I popped one into the VCR, and there was Shirley.

She wears her nurse's uniform and a safari helmet with a bug net attached. She steps into her front yard, which sits in a mosquito infested wetland, to watch her grandsons launch a rocket. Her face is barely visible through the bug netting, but her laughter rings out like wind chimes. In the background, I see her flower garden is in its early stage. The video must be ten years old then, because her gardens are glorious now. She weeded them herself until July, when she simply could not do it anymore. The safari helmet ultimately landed on her bedpost where, even when she was terribly sick, she managed to secure it on her head when the occasional bat got in. Shirley had an elaborate hairdo, perfect for bats to nest in. It even had a name: the Gibson Girl. Against all fashion trends, Shirley had worn the same style for twenty years, ever since her early forties. Maintaining it required brush rollers, bobby pins, hair spray. It was one of the last things she let go.

I keep one of her tortoise shell hairpins in my purse now.

In the end, I decide to attend the lunch. I drive past the True Vine, whose parking lot is full this week. I think of this as a good sign. But when I get to the Baha'i Center, I notice I am nervous and filled with dread. I step out of the sunlight into a large room at the precise moment at which a door opens across from me and children charge in, waving religious posters which they have just made in Sunday school. The parents, sitting in a circle, welcome them.

Personally, when I was young, I despised religious training, two hours' release time from public school every Wednesday for indoctrination by shriveled Catholic nuns. From the first Sunday that I was away from my parents' house, it never occurred to me, not once, to go to church. Shirley, on the other hand, was devout until thirty years ago, when she fell away for good reasons involving yet another bad priest, a priest who told falsehoods—some of them about Shirley. "She'll sleep with anybody who comes down the road in a pair of pants," he said, probably in a drunken stupor, to a loyal parishioner. "You're a goddamn lying bastard," this parishioner replied, enraged. And he was.

In truth, Shirley was prudish, and her only offense was being young and smart and beautiful and alone with six kids in a small-minded town. People talked viciously behind her back and smiled warmly at her on the communion line every Sunday. She couldn't stand it, and she stopped going to church. None of Shirley's children are Catholics. Only one, the youngest, Neal, is religious, and he is a relatively recent Mormon.

Lunch will soon begin, but before it does a woman, grey haired, accented, and mysterious, comes to welcome me. "Are you a seeker?" she asks me, point blank. What do I say? I am a Sunday seeker, a Sunday anthropologist? Should I simply announce to her that I'm searching for the spirit, searching for Shirley, searching for information about where she might be right now?

"I guess I'm a seeker," I mumble. I am seeking something, but, really, is it God? Earlier today, my friend Michele asked me if I was searching for a church to join. I quickly said no.

I said, "I don't know what I'm doing."

Secretly, though, I suspect that I am counting on Sunday church to keep me from being sucked into the past, into the dust of those seven months at the end of the dirt road. It is so easy to slide backward to Shirley's death, to the helplessness I felt as she wasted away before me.

I feel all of this, intensely, when I do not say, "I'm here because my sister just died, because I watched her die, and even though she believed in God, Jesus Christ to be specific, I don't." I don't even feel tempted to say it. And then another woman takes me over, an intense woman who's more than ready to answer my questions.

> We believe all prophets are messengers from one God.
> The last prophet was Baha'u'llah. Born in Persia. 1817.
> The Baha'i faith is 154 years old. Years young.
> There is no clergy. (To lie about you.)
> We teach tolerance.
> Every Baha'i is a student and a teacher.
> If you want to join, sign this, mail it in, and you will be
> placed on the roll.
> No, we don't believe in reincarnation, but we believe the
> consciousness and memory stay intact when you move
> on.

I am led to the bookstore, past pictures of their prophets and their holy sites in Haifa, where I buy two books. *Some Answered Questions* by Abdul-Baha and *Wings of Prayer: Baha'i Prayers for Women*. We eat: basmati rice, green salad, fruit. There is chicken curry, too. A five-dollar donation is requested, but they refuse my money. Enrolled members of the Baha'i faith pay; seekers don't. The Baha'i woman, in conversational style, instructs me throughout lunch.

> We believe that the world is changing toward total unity of
> all people.
> That we are all one.
> That each person is responsible for her own spiritual life.
> We teach but never proselytize. Our missionaries are called
> pioneers.

When Shirley was about twenty, she met Tom Dooley, a Catholic missionary and doctor who was on his way back to Africa, and he asked her to go with him. Though she wanted to, she didn't. Shirley got married instead, had six children. She told me several times that she knew her marriage was a mistake from the very first day, and she always wondered if she had missed her one chance, her true calling, and put herself on the wrong path when she said no to Africa and Dr. Tom Dooley.

Yet most people who met her thought of her as magical and even holy. She called herself a spiritual being on a human journey. She spread love everywhere she went. "Our angel," they called her in the nursing home where she worked.

"Do you have angels in Baha'i?" I suddenly ask, but she doesn't hear me, this woman, who is preparing to leave before the two "travelers" talk. The travelers, women in their fifties, are video-makers. They explain the principles of Baha'i, they say, in a right-brain way through images they capture on video in their travels. I watch their videos closely. I see people of all races and ages together, images of nature and Planet Earth. There is world music and poetry on the sound track. The spiritual quest is hard, the videos seem to say, but worth it. God is good, and the world, our world, is careening toward a change. The end is near. This life, life as we know it, is ending, and the future will be better. Much better. Here on Planet Earth.

Before the videos began, people in the audience produced spontaneous prayers. They asked for happiness, for freedom, for safety, for guidance, for love. They said these prayers in English and Spanish. Some were almost poems and started with words like, "I am a bird with a broken wing." And then the videos. And then a little discussion. And then it's over. On my way home, I think about prophets and prophecy. It interests me that prophets supposedly reveal the truth, the Truth, but they don't predict when it will come to pass. Prophets do not prophesize the future, like fortune tellers, and no matter how long ago they lived, they don't explain the past, either. Or the present. And we're still waiting for the Golden Rule to swing into effect.

During Stage Two of the Final Dive, for no reason, Shirley suddenly became terrified of going to hell. "You're not going to hell; you're going to heaven," we insisted. "You've done everything there is to do in your religion: confession, communion, the last rites. You lived a beautiful life, spread love, never sinned." But nothing helped. "I have to burn more," my sister whispered, many times. "Purgatory is O.K," she reassured us, wild eyed. Finally, we called Hospice and asked for anti-anxiety medication. We called it "sleep water." During this phase, Shirley asked, repeatedly, for just two things: "Fresh water and God. Fresh water, in my mouth. And God. Fresh water and God. Everyone else leave. Just fresh water stay. Fresh water and God." We were dropping water into her mouth by the teaspoonful. With a syringe the size of an eye dropper. Fresh water. Sleep water. And God.

Soon after that, she stopped talking.

Wednesday

Last night, I attended "Light Motion," the fourth dance concert in the KiMo series. The main attraction was a pair of women dancers: Joanne Petroff, who is able-bodied, and Charlene Curtiss, who dances in her wheelchair. The program says that "her original dance techniques in 'front-end chair control' have redefined dance parameters and choreographic techniques in wheelchair movement work." I didn't even know there *were* choreographic techniques in wheelchair movement work. But the second the lights dim, I am transfixed. Like a comet, Charlene Curtiss streaks across the stage in her customized wheelchair. She whirls around, balances on two wheels, and even tips it completely over and pitches herself out of it, backwards, onto the stage. She flies, really. And Joanne Petroff eggs her on, grabbing her hand and sending her rolling, speeding, careening toward the edge of the stage. She lies down and Charlene Curtis rolls her wheelchair right over her.

"Why dance concerts?" Sharon Oard Warner, a writer friend, has asked me over lunch. Last week, when I dropped into her office to say hello, she made the mistake of asking me the one question guaranteed to send me into a tailspin: How are you? I collapsed onto her couch and sobbed that, one recent morning, I woke up whispering, "Fresh water and God," words I had not thought of for almost two weeks, though during Stage Two of the Final Dive, I was certain they were burned into my short and long term memory for life.

"I can't bear it," I said. "Forgetting is worse than remembering."

Sharon's eyes filled with tears. Mine did, too. For minutes, we both quietly cried. Salt water, not fresh water. No God. Maybe God.

"Do you go to church?" I suddenly ask, and she shakes her head.

"For seven years, I went a lot, almost every Sunday," I say, "when I lived in L.A. and worked in the movie business. But it was a temple of tarot." We laugh, but the truth is, that temple and the work I did studying the esoteric meaning of tarot cards did more to revise my life for the better than fifteen years, off and on, of expensive psychotherapy. But then, somehow, mysteriously, it fizzled out for me. I don't even know where my tarot cards are, the deck I hand-painted, which took me a whole year.

Yet when Sharon asks me, "Why dance concerts?" I immediately think of the World, the final card, or key, in the Major Arcana of tarot. In it, an androgynous figure stands suspended in thin air, holding a spiral rod in each hand. It represents balance, integrity, mastery.

"Because I think life is a dance," I answer. That figure in Key Twenty-One has always looked to me like s/he's dancing. "I think of myself as in the dance or out of it; I notice if I feel in step or out of step. If I'm graceful or clumsy. If I'm stiff or loose and..."

I go to the dance concerts, I realize in this instant, to remind myself that other dances have continued on while I was far off the mainstream stage, doing the Death Dance with Shirley.

When I arrive home, there is a birthday card in the mail for me from my friend Madalyn. The watercolor painting on the card, by Melissa Harris, is of a woman leaping against pure blue-black indigo space, toward the moon. In tarot, Key Two, the Moon, symbolizes the memory. Under it, Madalyn has written, by hand, with a fountain pen, "Julie Mars! Dancing into her new life!"

I look at this painting for a very long time.

The First Unitarian Church of Albuquerque
Albuquerque, NM

I decide on the First Unitarian Universalist Church. The taped phone announcement informs callers that the Sunday service begins at eleven; the topic of the sermon is "The Mysteries of Love and Friendship," with the Reverend Christine Robinson presiding; the Chalice Singers will perform. I'm happy about this because I have been waiting three weeks now for live music, but when I mention it to my friend and neighbor Julie Reichert and she says, tactfully, "Don't expect Aretha Franklin," I experience a little stab of spiritual pessimism. It is still with me, a half hour later, when I pull into the huge parking lot, which is full past capacity. I have to cut through to an adjacent lot and park in front of a biotech company. People flood toward the door, sweeping me along. Inside is a table with name tags, pre-printed and blank, which I ignore. It bothers me, this idea that I must reveal my name, offer this clue to my identity to church-going strangers.

There are a few hundred or more people here, though I see only two people of color: one black woman and, several rows behind her, one black baby, sitting on a white woman's lap. On the front wall are various painted religious symbols: the yin/yang circle, the I Ching combinations, a cross, a Jewish star, the Islamic crescent moon and star, blank tablets pre-shaped for the Ten Commandments, the letters "IHS," even Boolean Circles, which I associate only with the library orientation tour I took at UNM when I returned to graduate school. I look around, fairly shamelessly, my eye catching again and again on a man in the row behind me, maybe seven seats over.

I think it is Peter Fonda.

I pretend to look past him at the quilt art on the wall, but I study his face carefully. He knows I'm looking at him but does not turn away. Instead, we stare straight at each other without any form of mutual acknowledgement. In this vacuum, I slip backward through the years, and there he is, riding his motorcycle on-screen in *Easy Rider*. I widen my view to include Shirley, sitting beside me in a darkened theatre in Colorado Springs. My friend Lizzie and I had hitchhiked out to see her at the Air Force Academy, where her husband taught. We were stopped at the gate. "There are two...uh...individuals here to see you," the Air Force policeman said to Shirley on the phone. We wore fringed jackets, headbands, no bras. I carried my belongings in a flowered, slipcover pillow case onto which I had sewn the legs of old blue jeans as shoulder straps. On the very first night, we begged Shirley to take us to the movies in her VW bug. We had already seen *Easy Rider*, of course—it was mandatory in our hippie culture—but I wanted Shirley to experience it, too. I wanted her to know me, her hippie sister, just turned eighteen. I'd finally broken out, escaped from the parental unit, and I was giddy with freedom. I carried the *Meditations of Marcus Aurelius* in my back pocket, and was prepared to live my life as a panhandler, if necessary.

During that visit, I talked non-stop. Downstairs in the basement, while Shirley ironed, I tried to explain how rejecting everything I came from and all that had happened to me up to that moment in life was crucial to my survival. "I'm like a spring that's just been pressed down for my whole life," I said, "and I've just sprung. I don't know when I'll stop bouncing."

"I hope you're not taking drugs," she said as she creased the sleeve of her husband's Air Force uniform.

"Nah, nothing serious, maybe a little pot and hash, maybe some mushrooms or acid. Nothing serious." I remember how she did not respond, how the steam rose off the ironing board in little white puffs. I left there knowing I could tell her anything, and she would not judge me or reject me. That acceptance gave me a place to stand.

When I resurface at the Unitarian Church, Peter Fonda's head is cocked to one side and he has a look of wonderment on his face. I turn away from him, toward the choirmaster, who announces that, in honor of Black History Month, we will sing rousing gospel songs instead of meditating before the service. But hardly anyone sings. I can barely hear the Chalice Singers, who are seated just four rows ahead of me, as we segue from "I'm Gonna Lay Down My Sword and Shield" into "Let Freedom Spin" and then "Every Time I Feel the Spirit." I am relieved when it's over.

The minister, Christine Robinson, comes out in an emerald green robe, like Key Three, the Empress, in tarot. A candle is lit. There's another hymn. And then the whole congregation joins in a "responsive affirmation." Of course, I say it, too:

> Love is the doctrine of this church;
> The quest for truth is its sacrament
> And service is its prayer.
>
> This is our covenant:
> To dwell together in peace,
> To seek knowledge in freedom,
> To serve Humanity in fellowship,
> To the end that all souls shall grow
>   into harmony with the divine.

There's a song in Spanish and a puppet show for the children and then we, the visitors, are asked to stand up and introduce ourselves. I do not, and neither does Peter Fonda. A "Pulpit Editorial" follows, in which a nervous member of the congregation speaks out against the death penalty. A bill for its repeal has just been defeated in our state legislature, and this speaker urges us to sign a petition. Systematically, he refutes the four major arguments in favor of capital punishment, and then wraps up by quoting Clarence Darrow. Everyone claps. Peter Fonda claps. Me? I am polite in my applause but honestly I don't see it the way other people do, maybe because I've spent years in prison. (Working.) I see death as relief for those poor, misguided, damaged criminals; a way for them to get on with it, on to their next incarnation, which will, hopefully, be a better one. At least, I used to feel this way, before the dying person was my sister and my doubts about the likelihood of a next incarnation began.

Just now, in this moment, I realize what my main problem is: Before I got up close and personal with death, I genuinely believed that the spirit went happily on into the afterlife. But when she died, Shirley just seemed dead. Deader'n a bag of hammers, as they say in the North Country of upstate New York. And I felt, and I feel, that her spirit died with her.

I am so bowled over by this that I barely hear the Chalice Singers perform "Go Down Moses," and I don't participate in the meditation in four forms: words, silence, song, and sharing. During the reading of Eugene Kennedy's *On Being a Friend,* though, I take out a pen and jot down a sentence: Death is the sinew and bone of all the other mysteries. I am too disturbed to decipher it and therefore grateful when Reverend Robinson begins to speak.

She begins by dividing mysteries into two categories: temporary ones, which can be solved with logic or luck, and existential ones, which are not to be solved but to be lived in. She talks about the risks of opening up, of being seen and known by others, of needing acceptance. And then she talks about the risk of letting go. Letting go of loved ones, perhaps because someone moves away, she says, is one way we prepare for our own final goodbye.

She says "letting go" many times in the sermon.

She also muses on the beauty and the necessity of separation, how we can only be truly intimate when we fully respect one another's need for distance. Giving one another the necessary space, she says, is the essence of love.

Space. Privacy. Love.

I did not ask Shirley if she wanted me to come back east to take care of her. I just decided to go, even knowing that she was an intensely, fiercely private person. In fact, when she called me to tell me that her cancer diagnosis was official, that the blood test for cancer markers in the pancreatic enzymes that I, not her doctor, had ordered had come back dirty, I told her I would pack up immediately and she said, "Not yet. I don't need you yet. I promise I will let you know when I need you." But Shirley never let anyone know when she needed anything, so I ignored her. Quit my job. Left New Mexico.

I drove east with my husband, Robert, whose life since he came with me to New Mexico had seemed as parched to him as the desert we now lived in. He was fed up and was planning to move back to our house in upstate New York anyway. In a motel in Joplin, Missouri, when the lights were out and the only sound was the rattle of the air conditioner, he took my hand and said, "I know you're not going back because of me. I know the only reason you're going is because Shirley is sick. Let's just have that out in the open."

I held my breath. Said nothing.

We both knew our marriage was out of gas again, running on fumes. At such times, we usually separate for a while to regroup. We calm down, and wait it out.

But this time that could not happen.

"I know you don't want me here bugging you," I said to Shirley when I arrived, "but here I am." She shook her head. "It's not like I have anything better to do, you know." She shook her head again, but later (months later), she took my hand and said, "I accept this from you." Her son Jimmy and I became her health care proxies, and she gave us power of attorney. I signed on with Hospice as her primary caretaker. She thanked me for my help every single day, just before she fell asleep.

In the beginning, I checked in on Shirley every afternoon, cooked for her, ran errands, fielded phone calls, sent people away from the door. I went away myself, back to my own house late at night unless, rarely, she asked me to stay. Knowing I had violated her wish to be left alone, I worked hard to stay behind the ropes she had set up—psychically, spiritually, and emotionally—and I tried to keep others out of her space for her. None of this was easy. People resented me. One of Shirley's friends, a woman who called her several times a day (Shirley hated the phone) and to whom I was always polite, called me a barnyard dog. I hurt everyone—her kids, her sisters, her friends—when I sent out an e-mail saying: Shirley wants your phone calls limited to ten minutes once a week. She doesn't want to talk about her health. She wants, only, to hear your news. I had to do it because Shirley, who lived at the end of a dirt road like a hermit, was suddenly inundated with well-wishers, and she was overwhelmed. It shocked her: the constant bouquets, the daily cards, the frequent visitors. The concern. The love. It wore her out.

But for us, it was excruciating to give her space.

At the very end, two weeks before she died, she whispered in my ear, "All that stuff I said about just wanting to die in peace with no one around? I don't feel that way anymore. I don't want to be alone anymore."

My sister was never alone again after that, except for a few hours on Christmas day, when my niece Julie and I took a two-hour car ride through the snowy countryside. We left her then, deep into Stage Three, because we thought that maybe she needed to be alone after all to die. On that day, she had not eaten for fifteen days. She had not had a drop of water for eight. Her body was like a machine: heart and lungs rhythmically pumping. "I have a strong heart and lungs. That's my problem," Shirley had thoughtfully said in Stage One of the Final Dive. I heard her words over and over again as I watched the flutter of her heart beneath her chest.

So we left a note on the door, asking whoever came to give her a little space. And we scraped the snow and ice off the car, climbed in, and drove away. We made a big circle: Bombay, Massena, Potsdam, back to Moira. It was the strangest drive I've ever taken. Both of us were edgy. When we returned and peeked into her room, Shirley was still there. In Stage Three. Breathing. About three times a minute.

There is a final hymn in the Universalist service during which I have to hold hands with two people I don't know. I dislike this, even if I am on a mission to find the spirit. As I walk back to my car, I feel upset. I have always believed that the world is just, that every person in it somehow receives exactly the lessons that he or she needs for personal evolution. But I cannot make this concept match up to my sister's suffering and death. She was a good person, a beautiful person, yet, in the end, she didn't get a single thing she wanted, except to die at home. She wanted to die quickly, not to linger, but she lingered for months. "I don't want to be hanging around for Thanksgiving and Christmas, wrecking everybody's holidays," she said, but she made it by twenty minutes through both. She wanted to take care of herself until she died, but in the end she was totally helpless. She wanted to take care of our parents, which she described as her last big job in life. Instead, they outlived her. She called them and each of her six kids and each sister to say goodbye at the beginning of Stage One of the Final Dive. Our sister Laurie dialed the phone and held it to Shirley's ear while I sat, rigid, in the kitchen, my fingers digging into the fabric of the armchair her kids had just given her for her last Mother's Day.

One by one, Shirley made those calls. Ten different goodbyes.

There was nothing fair about it.

How can things like that happen, I'm wondering. If there is a God, there must be something seriously wrong with Him, Her, or It. A decent God could not allow so much suffering to descend on a beautiful person like Shirley. A person who spent her whole life giving to others.

I start the car and drive slowly across the lot. I can actually feel my heart pumping red rage though my body. As I wait to turn south onto Carlisle, I notice a sign by the entrance to the Universalist church. "Unanswered questions are far less dangerous than unquestioned answers," it says.

Wednesday

Last night at seven, the phone rang. It was my friend, another Julie, Julie Shigekuni. "I have my baby girl," she said, and I stammered, "You do? You do?"

"You want to come and see her?"

"Can I?"

"Yes, come." She asked me to bring her a vanilla milkshake and a sandwich from the Route 66 Diner, which is right across the street from Presbyterian Hospital, where she rested on the third floor. I sat there, on the take-out bench, in a time warp: music from the fifties, hopscotch built into the floor tiles, big comfortable booths, old Route 66 signs, waitresses in bobby socks and crisp turquoise uniforms.

Shirley had her first baby in the fifties. Billy was born in Enid, Oklahoma, when Shirley was twenty-one. A year later, Julie was born at West Point, the U. S. Military Academy, where our father taught physical education and unarmed combat for thirty years. We lived in Quarters

Six. Shirley was staying with us, waiting for her baby. Right after Julie was born, she flew to Okinawa, where her husband was stationed. She lived there for two years, and had another baby, Johnny.

The Army Hospital where my niece was born was a short bike ride from our house, but children like me were not allowed in the maternity ward. Instead, I stood in the parking lot or on the hill behind the hospital and threw gravel at the window. Shirley would eventually appear there, her long hair pinned up in front but falling over her shoulders. Through the thick screen, I could see the vague shape of her newborn baby, Julie, in her arms, wrapped in a pink blanket. Shirley would wave. I wanted to shout, "I miss you," but yelling was not allowed in the hospital zone.

When I enter the hospital room of this Julie, my friend, the lights are low and she is propped up in bed with her new daughter. Issa is less than four hours old when I walk in the door. Julie looks bright-eyed, beautiful. Her long black hair is collected into a ponytail that trails down her back. Her smile is endless as she shifts her newborn daughter so I can see her. "Isn't she pretty?" she asks.

"She's gorgeous," I say, and I mean it. I am actually stunned at the perfection of this little being, four hours old, whose mother is starving, ravenous. Julie hands me the baby and tears into her milkshake and sandwich. I call forth all my baby-holding moves. My older sisters— Joanie, Shirley, Mary, and Janet—had babies constantly. Among them, they had seventeen. And my younger sister, Laurie, had three. I am the only one in the family who just said no to motherhood. Because there have always been babies, I know enough to support her neck and back, but even as I take Issa from Julie, I am secretly terrified that I might do something wrong, maybe drop her or crush her or not notice, in the dim room, that she is not breathing right. Maybe lose my mind and forget I'm holding her when I stand up.

Issa is so incredibly light in my arms. Not even seven pounds. She is swaddled tightly and wears a white knit hat with a red pompom. I stare into her little round face. She has a tiny nose and a rosebud mouth. Her skin is amazingly soft, with tiny patches of pink and orange in it. Her eyes are closed.

Julie, sitting on an ice pack, drinks her milkshake and then gets up to adjust the lights. I can hardly believe she gave birth four hours ago.

To this little being in my arms. She gazes at Issa with eyes that shine.

"It's a miracle," I say.

"It is," Julie answers.

Julie needs rest, and it's only two hours until Issa's next feeding. "I need to sleep a little, but I want her to be held," she says. "Will you hold her for me while I sleep?"

It's an honor for me.

"It's an honor and a privilege," I said when people asked me why I went east to take care of Shirley.

I adjust the chair and settle in while Julie closes her eyes. Soon, within two minutes, her breath lengthens. I am hypnotized by this baby in my arms. Her face is like the moon in the dim light. Her face is like the sea. Her face is like time. I can't stop staring into it. Issa's little fist is raised to the side of her head in a power salute. She is impossibly tiny in my arms.

Shirley loved babies and old people. I remember standing at the door of her bedroom before she broke my heart and left for Okinawa, watching her love her two babies. She wrapped them in laughter and gentleness. I was eight years old, in the doorway. "Come in," she'd say to me. I would run in and climb onto the bed. Press up next to her. She would hold one baby, and I would hold the other. Usually, Shirley would hum. When she took those babies and disappeared, I had a black hole in my chest.

It feels so right, so excellent, to be in this dim room with my friend Julie asleep in the bed and her daughter in my arms. It seems perfect, really, if I don't count my fear of doing something wrong. But just before an hour is up, Issa starts screaming. I am shocked at the racket. I stand up and try to bounce her into quietness, but it doesn't work and soon Julie wakes up.

"You didn't even get to sleep an hour," I say regretfully as I give her back her baby.

"It was enough," she says. And she does look completely refreshed, even glowing. I am baffled by this. The baby continues to scream.

"Can't the nurses take care of her?" I ask, because I know Julie needs more rest.

"She screams, and I respond. It's part of bonding," Julie tells me. She is so matter of fact about everything in life that sometimes she scares me. "We're in for a long night, aren't we, Issa?" she coos. "You're disturbed, aren't you, baby?" She looks up at me. "She's two weeks early, you know. She's not really happy about being here so soon."

I nod as if I get it. Motherhood.

Shortly afterward, I leave.

Mother and daughter, doing fine.

It is magical, this cold desert night. I can't stop smiling, though basically I'm not a smiler. I look tense and anxious most of the time, not happy, not smiling, like Julie. And Shirley. On the drive home, I pass by the Artichoke Cafe, where I had my birthday dinner just last night.

Yesterday, I turned fifty.

To celebrate, I took an ex-student of mine, now a friend, a young Vietnamese woman who has the same birthday as I do, out to this expensive restaurant for dinner. Last year, before Shirley got sick and I went east, Ut used to come to my office to work on her papers for English 102. We fell into a lovely pattern: she would come for an hour or more a few times a week, before my pottery class. We would work on her essay for a while, but somehow, magically, she would begin to tell me stories about her early life in Vietnam. Her stories would transport me there, to the river where women threw in their unwanted American babies, and to the cemetery on the edge of which Ut lived. Into the house where they locked the doors and windows against the ghosts each night at sundown. Once, she told me how she had had to quit school in the fourth grade to work. She desperately wanted to continue her education, and an old woman who lived nearby made her a deal: if Ut would pluck the grey hairs from her head, this woman would teach her arithmetic and other subjects. Every night, Ut did this. Later, she won an all-Vietnam scholastic contest.

She has just applied to the pharmacy program at UNM.

During dinner, which she barely touched, we talked about the Buddhist temple she has started to visit almost every night. Ut says that she is terribly happy in the temple. She loves to go there and wash the dishes. She says that she sometimes wants to become a nun. "If you're a nun, you can get your whole family into heaven after they die," she says. But if you're a pharmacist, you can take care of them on earth. She is going to Vietnam this summer, her first visit. Her family has saved four-thousand dollars, enough money to build her grandmother a house. Her grandmother's house washed away in a flood last year.

"Can you be a Buddhist nun and a pharmacist, too?"

Ut just laughed at me.

Later, after dinner, when I got home, I felt somewhat misaligned and out of sorts. I kept thinking about our $54 dinner, put on my credit card. When Ut arrived in the restaurant, I was already seated.

"Here we are, hanging out with the rich and famous on our birthday," I had joked as she sat down.

"Being together is the richness," she answered, lovely in a red dress and high heels that made her nearly as tall as I am.

Over Shirley's last months, I learned many lessons—or was reminded of them. Sometimes they felt like punches, uppercuts into my status quo, and sometimes they felt like little ringing bells. When it was my time to speak, during her memorial service, I mentioned four specific ones. The first one, the one Shirley lived by the most, even at the end when she applied it to her morphine, was: Don't take more than you need.

I didn't need that $54 dinner, and neither did Ut.

I knew this beforehand but I wanted to do something special for Ut, who made it, beautifully and against many odds, to twenty-one. Who just today sent in her application to pharmacy school. Just today, I contacted my former agent in New York, and told her I had finished the novel, *Anybody Any Minute*, that I had started several years ago. Every evening, for seven months, after Shirley climbed into bed, I read her my new pages. "Where does it come from?" she asked, over and over. "I don't know," I always answered, truthfully. She told me that the characters in my book were the last friends she would ever make. I wanted to make them wonderful for her. I finished the draft just before she took the Final Dive. Together, and laughing, we composed the words to the dedication: This book is dedicated to the memory of my sister Shirley, who wanted it on the record that she did not approve of certain parts.

We had many things to celebrate on our birthday, Ut and I, but in the end, ignoring the don't-take-more-than-you-need lesson I learned, at a very high price, put a damper on the party. Let me make this clear: I do not care one bit about the money. It's not the money. It's the feeling that Ut was uncomfortable there. It's the memory of the way she held her thin red jacket closed tightly in front of her, her hand clenched along the lapel, that bothers me. It makes me wonder why I didn't ask her to take me to her favorite Vietnamese diner instead.

Albuquerque Friends Meeting
Albuquerque, NM

This week, the Quakers.

All my associations with Quakers are positive: they were conscientious objectors during Vietnam. When I was in college, a professor of nineteenth-century British literature whom I considered to be evolved, enlightened, and wise, was a Quaker. One of my sister Mary's sons is married to a woman raised a Quaker, and she is warm, animated, and fun-loving. I actually look forward to going. Arrive early.

I have heard that the service centers on silent meditation. "My guess is that everyone just sits there until somebody skinny boils over," I tell Julie Reichert when she asks me about my expectations. Honestly, I have meant to go to a Quaker meeting ever since the Vietnam days, but it has taken me thirty years to get here.

A woman holds the door open for me, smiles, and says hello. Across the tiny lobby, I see a large room with chairs in four concentric circles. Many people are seated inside already, so I enter and settle in the middle row. It is absolutely quiet in this room: white walls, open windows, no art, no prophets' pictures, no nothing. I see one girl, a teenager with long, straight hair, writing in a notebook between glances around the group.

Most people have closed their eyes, and many heads have fallen forward onto chests. Old men and women look sleepy. Everyone is white. It is intensely quiet, with only car sounds from outside filtering in through the windows. And in the distance, a little Mexican music.

This continues for many minutes. No one boils over. Actually, it's peaceful, and I feel myself calming. It occurs to me that I have no idea what I should be doing. Thinking about God? Examining my conscience? Praising the Lord? I don't even know if the Friends agree on who-is-God. There are no pictures, and none of the usual religious reading material in the lobby.

After a while, I notice that I can describe what kind of shoes everyone in my row is wearing, so I figure I must have been staring down, toward the floor, for quite some time. I hear chairs creak and stomachs growl, but no one says a single word. No one smiles either but suddenly I do, thinking that the Friends don't seem too friendly. We look, as a group, a little world weary. I glance around at all the bowed heads. I bow mine.

Suddenly, I find myself reflecting on something that happened to me two mornings ago. I say "happened to me" because I did not ask for it, and I did not want it. It came to me on its own. I woke up that day, and despite the little black Chinese pills that Alexcia has given me for the free-floating anger that often wakes me at night, I was enraged because, way back in September, after Shirley had just had her session with the faith healer, Paul Timmons, everyone (assuming she was on the road to wellness) disappeared for six weeks, leaving me alone with her. It was a good time, her upward surge, when her symptoms seemed to reverse themselves and she began to eat, gain weight, and sleep comfortably on her back for the first time in months. But then, after three weeks, she plummeted. Down, down, down. She agonized, relentlessly, about having asked to be healed, about whether she deserved it, about whether she really wanted it or had just done it to please everyone else. She had asked for a miracle, but it hadn't come on her terms—or ours. We wanted total recovery on the spot. It looked, instead, like if she recovered at all, she would have to inch her way painfully back to health.

For a while, she tried.

Every day, she walked (her posture, perfect) around the kitchen table, into the living room, around the coffee table, back into the kitchen. Four times in a row, three times a day. She made herself eat. She took alternative medicines that a former student of mine, a Japanese man named Kenshin, found for her on the Internet. It was so much work for Shirley, trying to get well. But then she stopped wanting to work so hard. She got deeply, terrifyingly depressed. She stopped bathing and combing her hair. She politely told me and her son Jimmy to go away. She said she didn't care about anything anymore.

I didn't know what to do, so I reported it all to our wonderful Hospice nurse, Mary Lou. Many years before, when she was a nurse's aide, Shirley trained Mary Lou in the nursing home. Mary Lou said Shirley was one of the people who had put her on her path, who changed the course of her life. When Shirley got sick, Mary Lou volunteered to take her on as a special case. This meant she came before she started her on-call schedule every day. She came, often on her own time, outside of her work hours, which were four p.m. to eight a.m., five days a week.

"She has every right to be depressed," Mary Lou said. "She's very sick." She was throwing up twenty times a day, everything she ate. Jaundiced. Starving. Weak.

"I know, I know," I said, "but…"

But this wasn't Shirley.

This problem was way out of my league. Looking back on it, it was infinitely worse than the Final Dive.

And no one came to help me. I asked, I thought I asked, over and over again. But no one came.

I would get home at night and cry, hysterically. Shirley does not go into the Black Hole, I said to Robert. She doesn't. Such a thing was incomprehensible to me. Shirley never slid into the darkness (like I used to), but now she had. She wouldn't wash her face or let me change her sheets. She refused to take the vitamins I had started her on during the good weeks after the healing. She put away her photo albums and watched *The Bold and the Beautiful* instead. Half watched. She said she had to get back to where she was before. "I was almost there," she said, her brown eyes stormy. "I was ninety percent there."

Among the Friends of Albuquerque, I think about this. How I had woken up, two days before, fuming that nobody came to help me during those six weeks. I relive it, I feel my heart pound, but I don't boil over.

Nobody does.

The only words happen forty-five minutes into the meeting when a mother and a child, a toddler, enter the room. When she closes the door behind her, this baby boy squirms out of her arms and tries to reach the doorknob to escape. He can't, and he says to her, his mother, in strangely correct English, "Hey! What're you doing?"

I laugh. It's a good question, kid.

I, for one, don't have the first idea what I'm doing.

It has started to seem airless in the room, and suddenly it smells sweaty. But it's peaceful, and when I open my eyes, I catch a little movement, some waviness in my peripheral vision, as if something has floated away, just out of my line of sight. I turn my head, but there's nothing there. And then I notice that I do not feel mad at anyone about those six weeks last fall, including myself. I was so mad at myself for being incompetent. So mad at everyone else for being oblivious. So mad at the world for being cruel. So mad at Shirley for dying.

Once, in Stage Two of the Final Dive, my niece Julie and I were trying to make Shirley comfortable, to medicate her, to cover the places where her skin was breaking down with a kind of medicinal Saran Wrap called Tegaderm. "Why can't you just let it be what it is?" Shirley suddenly asked, as if she had just climbed up on an island in her sea of incoherence. "I've never been madder," she added, and Julie and I laughed. Shirley was mad at us because we wouldn't just let it be what it was. Her dying.

A few minutes later, the Friends of Albuquerque reach for one another's hands, squeeze, and then let go. A few people make announcements—about helping earthquakes victims in El Salvador and in India, or about meeting plans. And then each person says his or her name. Another round of hand squeezing. And it's over.

No mention of God, nor the spirit, nor the principles of Quakerhood. No preaching, no singing, no talking, no smiling. I think about last week's sermon on friendship. The minister said friends give each other privacy and space.

Of space and privacy, there is plenty here in this room.

On my way out the door, I think I would've done better with an instruction booklet of some kind, some printed matter that told me, specifically, what to do. But as I sit in the car and watch the Friends emerge from the meeting house, to hop onto bicycles and peddle away or stroll down the block in the sun or climb into cars, I feel not-mad, and I begin to think that I did some small version of the right thing after all.

Thursday

Before I began my *Month of Sundays*, I wrote this:

I am driving on Route 11, through West Bangor, in my sister Shirley's 1995 Ford Escort. It is winter. For two months, the sky has been white. The snow is white across fields that stretch all the way to the St. Lawrence River and beyond, into Canada. No matter how carefully I look, there is no horizon line. Just endless white. It makes me think of paste, as if this world is pasted together with flour and water, sculpted into snowdrifts and plow piles and layers like frosting on top of the cars that pass me on the icy road.

I have a heavy heart accompanied by this strange insight: when approaching the inevitable, there is no fear. Instead, there is a funny halo of silence, a dampening, that insulates me from the sounds around me: the roaring car heater, trucks passing me, my breathing. My ears feel strange. I feel strange. I feel numb, like winter toes in winter boots, long past the tingling stage. Past the ache. A long, long time from the thaw.

I am driving to my sister Shirley's house, the last house on a dead-end dirt road, to watch her die. To comfort her while she's dying. To help her die, if I can. I have been coming here for almost seven months, almost every day. Many times, I come afraid. Is today the day? But now I know that when the last days are upon you, when you're in them, you know. There is no mistaking this. Then fear and wonder vanish. Tension vanishes. I feel myself hunkering down, steeling my nerves, trying to relax. I think, I have a job to do. Shirley has a job to do. We have an important job to do. It is important. This job.

I feel lonely.

I turn on the radio. Shirley's car has a good radio. In the summer, when she drives down her dirt road, she blasts it so loud that you can hear her coming from half a mile away. She loves music. She drives with the windows open to the wind and the music blaring. On the dashboard, I count three different pairs of sunglasses. Cheap sunglasses with huge frames and lenses that go from darker at the top to lighter at the bottom. She wears them over top of her own glasses. Many times I have looked at her and wondered how her nose can take all that weight across the bridge, how she can fit two pairs of glasses' legs behind her ears. Why she doesn't buy a pair of prescription sunglasses.

Shirley hasn't been in her car for three months now. She is disappearing, like a shadow in the path of the shade, from her own world. She can't make it to her flower garden. She can't make it to the sun porch. Even with her walker, she can't make it to the bathroom or the kitchen, even though her bedroom is just one step away. She lives in her bedroom now. She lives in a hospital bed provided by Hospice of the North Country instead of her 185-acre retreat, which she bought for $10,000, thirty years ago, when her husband, a bomber pilot, was sent to Vietnam—well, Thailand, actually.

Some music starts. A male voice, gentle and pure. He is singing "Somewhere over the Rainbow." Changing the words a little, not much. And filling Shirley's car with beauty. Route 11 is straight in this part, between Bangor and Brushton, and I notice that my grip on the steering wheel has loosened, just a little. This man, this singer, is reaching into me. I have seen videos of the psychic surgeons of the Philippines, and this is the same. And then the song shifts, and he's singing, "What a Wonderful World." This song, the Louis Armstrong version, is a song I listen to in the morning, many mornings, in lieu of morning prayers.

At least five miles disappear before the radio announcer says the singer's name. He is Hawaiian with a name that I can't begin to spell, though I have had the sense to find a pen and am prepared to write it down on my McDonald's napkin. The announcer says the singer is dead. Finally, she says the name of the CD: "Facing Future."

I don't cry when I hear that, even knowing that Shirley has almost no future left and I am about to face a future without her in it. I actually don't cry that much anymore. We cried, everybody cried, day and night in the beginning, seven months ago, when we finally got a diagnosis for her: pancreatic cancer. I was there, present in the room, when her doctor said, "It's a killer." And then she repeated it. "It's a killer." This doctor had been treating my sister for more than six months. For ulcers. I do not let myself think about this doctor very often.

It is Monday, December 11th, the day my sister Shirley took her Final Dive. For two long weeks, she plummeted downward, free-falling.

Falling free.

And I was there.

That version of "Somewhere over the Rainbow" was by Israel Kamakawiwo'Ole, otherwise known as "Iz K," a 750-pound Hawaiian who died young. When his voice filled Shirley's car, I became obsessed and immediately ordered the CD from Amazon.com, even though I did not have a CD player. Even though I didn't even know how to put a CD in a CD player, if I had one. I waited for it, tensely. I told Shirley about it when she was in Stage One of the Final Dive. I wanted her to hear that song.

When it came, she was already past listening. I opened the CD and my nephew Johnny showed me how to play it on my laptop computer. Robert, Shirley's kids, and I sat in the living room and, after the first few notes, we jumped to our feet and began to hula. We made big sweeping gestures above us to indicate the rainbow. We flapped our arms to look like "bluebirds, way up high." We developed hand and arm motions to mean lullaby, lemon drops, chimney tops. We played that song (my nephew Jimmy made a tape of it) a hundred times during the Final Dive. Everyone wanted a copy.

When Shirley died, Julie, Neal, and I knelt around her bed and Neal said a Mormon prayer. It was Christmas night, twenty minutes after twelve. My feet were jammed in under the visitor's chair and I got a charleyhorse in the middle of it, but I stayed put, looking at Shirley, brave Shirley, whose body we had straightened out and covered with the down comforter I bought for her (my last gift). I wondered where she was off to. Maybe somewhere over the rainbow.

Julie called her sister and other brothers and I called my sister Janet and Shirley's friend Marcia. Then Neal drove into town to tell Jimmy in person. When Neal left, Julie and I, without thinking twice, put "Somewhere over the Rainbow" into the tape player. We blasted it, top volume. We stood facing Shirley in her bed, shoulder to shoulder, and we did our whole routine. For her.

In the song, there is a line that says, "That's where you'll find me." We changed that to, "That's where we'll find *you*," and we both pointed at Shirley in perfect unison, like the Supremes. And when, in the "Wonderful World" part of the song, Iz K, sings, "they're really saying, I...I love you," Julie and I looked right into each other's eyes. We didn't turn it off until we saw headlights coming down the dirt road.

When Julie called her sister that night, Kimberly was not surprised that her mother had just passed. She had been sitting up late, in her home in Vermont, Christmas night, working on a crafts project.

At the very beginning of Stage Two, early one morning, Shirley woke up saying, "Cut me from here to here." She indicated her torso area. Obviously, she hurt, and badly. She kept mumbling, from the strange world of Stage Two, "I can't cut the string, I can't cut the string."

Julie was on one side of Shirley's bed, and I was on the other. "What string?" we asked.

"The one that's keeping me here."

"Where is it?"

"I don't know. Somewhere around here." She made a circle over her stomach area.

"Can't you find it and cut it, Shirley?" I asked again, because I really wanted her to be able to. No more pain, I was thinking.

"I can't find it," she said, a little angrily.

I said, "Julie, give me those scissors. I want to cut the string for Shirley." Julie reached behind her and handed me the scissors we used to cut the Tegaderm. I put my fingers through them. "I'm going to cut the string for you, Shirley," I said.

"Oh baloney," she replied.

Julie and I laughed. We put a bag of frozen peas on the area that hurt her. Sometimes the cold helped. And I gave her her rosary beads, hoping they would provide comfort in her hour of need.

"Get all this junk off me," Shirley said.

We laughed harder.

We told everyone this story, and everyone laughed. It was so incongruous, Shirley being miffed. The worst word she had said before, in her direst and most horrible pain, was "Gosh."

Many times, I looked at her, hard, trying to see the string that held her here.

A few days ago, I got a package from my niece, Kimmer: a framed photo of Shirley and her six kids on the day of the faith healing in September. A sympathy card for me, which touched me deeply. A copy of what everybody said at the memorial service.

And this, a story from Kim, which she had told me right after Shirley died. I had asked her to write it down and send it to me.

While I was at Mom's (the last time), I started a doily. Mom really wanted to see it done while I was there. She said she hoped I would finish it and not let another project go incomplete—but I just couldn't do it. I did finish it on December 17th or so—all except for cutting it away from the material.

December 25th: 11-12:15 at night. Our house. Bennington, Vermont.

I suddenly got a bit perturbed. O.K., Mom, I'll finish it. I'll do it. I'm cutting the strings, Mom. I'm cutting the strings. See? I'm going to finish this project.

My thoughts shifted. I became less perturbed and more tearful.

It's O.K., Mom. I'm cutting the strings. We're cutting the strings. We'll all be O.K. We love you. We're letting you go. We're cutting the strings.

It's time, Mom. You can go. We'll be O.K. We'll miss you but we'll be O.K.

Then, feeling ridiculous, I put the project down and headed into the other room. And this haltingly deep feeling comes over me. I stopped, closed my eyes, and rested my head against the wall. I realized I had started talking out loud. I was saying, "I know." I was answering Mom.

It wasn't her voice, but it was her saying:

"I love you." (I know, I know.)

"I'm proud of you." (I know, I know.)

"Always remember me." (I will, Mom. I will.)

"Always keep love in your heart." (I will, I will.)

And then I saw this far-off circle of light open up with Mom going toward it. There was light and circular, swaying movement. Suddenly, Mom came back down with this overwhelming warmth encircling me—hugging me. And then she moved slowly back up toward the light.

"God, your angel is home. Goodbye, Mom. I love you."

I went to bed. Five minutes later, up north in Moira, Mom died.

Kim says that, although she was the person who got it, she is positive that it was a message to all of us.

St. George Greek Orthodox Church
Albuquerque, NM

This week I am in the mood for smoke and mirrors, bells and whistles, robes and incense, so I choose the St. George Greek Orthodox church. I wear a plain green dress that Shirley made for me in my post-glamour phase and a sweater that she knit. I like driving slowly through parts of town that I have never seen, searching for random churches on Sunday.

The Greek Orthodox church sits in a quiet neighborhood filled with tiny houses. It is on the corner, surrounded by a high wall with wrought iron gates, and it mixes Southwest style—the creamy color, the high wall, the red-orange roof tiles—with Eastern features, like twin, gleaming gold basilicas with crosses atop each one. From my position on the street, it looks like breasts have been implanted onto a basic desert building. I am already parked near a pint-sized fire station when Father Mario, wearing sunglasses and carrying a gym bag, arrives to unlock the carved church doors. Besides me, there is no churchgoer in sight.

At five to nine, I leave the car. I have called ahead and listened to the tape. The voice said that [something Greek] begins at nine, so here I am. I step into an empty church. There is no altar—just a raised platform, the *solea,* carpeted in red. Across the front wall are beautiful, life-size icons of saints painted on wooden panels. Above these panels is a painting of the Last Supper and in the highest panel of all a big brown eye gazes out from the top third of a pyramid. After a few minutes, a second priest in a black cassock walks to the right side of the *solea,* places a fat book on the podium in front of him, and begins to sing. Then, dramatically, the center panel of the series of icons slides open to reveal the altar I noticed was missing. Father Mario circles it doing priestly jobs. The two priests are deeply involved in call-and-response prayer.

After ten minutes, a woman approaches me from behind and hands me a red looseleaf book. "So you can follow along," she whispers.

"Am I allowed to be here?" I whisper back, because until she arrived, it was just me and the two singing priests. "Of course," she answers, touching my arm. "These pages," she says showing me the first eleven pages, typed single spaced, "are for the first hour. And these are for the second."

The second? These Greeks don't mess around. I follow along, but chanting "Lord have mercy" can only hold my attention for so long. I begin to peruse the Sunday program and soon learn that this is Cheese Sale Sunday, the Sunday before the "Great Fast" dedicated specifically to forgiveness. The particular saint being honored is St. Porphyrius of Gaza. When he went to Egypt in 400 A.D., it says, there were only 280 Christians, "the rest of the inhabitants being fanatical idol-worshippers." I almost laugh out loud.

Last summer, Shirley's friend Marcia went to Egypt. When she returned with her pictures, she showed Shirley the pyramids at Giza. From the kitchen, I watched Shirley and Marcia study each photograph. That was a good day for my sister. When Marcia had left on her trip a few weeks before, I had promised to inform her by e-mail when Shirley died. We didn't think (nobody thought) Shirley would make it until Marcia returned. But then, Paul, the faith healer, came and somehow drew her away from Death's Door. For a little while.

"The temples of the idol worshippers were closed, the idols demolished, and a fine church built with thirty marble pillars," the story continues. St. Porphyrius died in 421, his relics "preserved in Gaza to this day." For the fanatical relic-worshippers, I think.

After about a half hour, two elderly women come, and then a middle-aged man who crosses the *solea,* opens a secret door among the icons, and disappears into a room beyond. In the few seconds that the door is open, I see racks of exotic, glittery satin vestments, and I sit up and crane my neck. These secret panels among the icons fascinate me. It's like being in an Agatha Christie mystery because, from this point forward, for not two but three hours, priests and altar boys (altar teens, actually) disappear into and out of these hidden doors constantly. Something important is going on back there—the sacred mystery, I assume—and we in the audience can only catch glimpses of it.

After the first hour, the church begins to fill up. Five men have joined the first singing priest and now they harmonize. Father Mario has changed his clothes again, and now wears gold and white satin vestments. A third priest has come on board for the service, wearing purple and gold, and the four altar teens shimmer in golden robes. The singing is continuous, and incense burns in fancy swinging holders. There is lots of kissing of the holy pictures, and, at one point, the priest carries a jeweled book from the altar and everyone—and the crowd is growing, exponentially—steps into the center aisle, lines up, and goes forward two by two to kiss it.

Father Mario continues to fuss behind the icon wall, though periodically he comes out and, with his entourage of golden teens, parades up and down the aisles, once with crosses and again with lanterns. Entranced women reach out to touch his robe when he passes along the aisle. And always, there is singing and incense, so much incense that the whole church is smoky.

By 10:30, the place is packed. People chat across the pews, and women are dressed to kill: feathered hats, skirts slit to the thigh, hair falling seductively across one eye. There is so much perfume that I get dizzy. Children, many per family, smack each other as they recite prayers. We vary between standing, sitting, and kneeling, and when a pregnant woman in front of me sits down abruptly during a kneeling part, an old woman behind me pokes me hard in the ribs and tells me to check to make sure she's all right. She is. She turns to the old woman. "I'm so ready to have this baby," she announces, "I might deliver it myself on the kitchen floor." I avert my eyes and listen to the chatter all around me, Greek and English, and the priests sing on.

About two hours in, there's a sermon during which Father Mario, like a wrathful God tempted to smite, yells at us non-stop. This is a far cry from the Quaker silence or the spiritual non-interference of the Universalists. With all the smoke and singing and the fire and brimstone rhetoric, I am very entertained and even moved. "It is Lent. DO SOME-THING!" Father Mario bellows. "If you have never done one thing for the salvation of your soul, DO SOMETHING! And if you think you have done everything you can possibly do, DO MORE!"

I actually begin to wonder what I can do. Shirley always gave up sweets for Lent, which for her was not so easy. She had a real sweet tooth. But after her symptoms started, she lost interest in sweets. She stopped drinking coffee, too—instant Taster's Choice in hot tap water. By the time I got back there in June, she was subsisting on red food only: raspberries, tomatoes, tomato soup. Later, near the end, she lived on cantaloupe. And fifteen days before she died, she gave up eating entirely.

Suddenly, the priest ends his tirade. He tosses his white cape back over his shoulders, revealing a crucifix which he clutches before his heart. Dramatically, he pauses for a few beats and then he says, quietly, "I can be a rotten person."

I hear the old woman behind me whisper to her friend, "He can."

"If I have done anything to offend any of you in this past year, I ask you to forgive me." He seems so humble now that I squeeze my eyes shut to keep from tearing up, and the rest of the service is a blur. I feel scraped raw inside. I keep seeing Father Mario looking us in the eye, admitting he's a rotten person, and asking for forgiveness.

Wednesday

Yesterday at five a.m., I lit my Shirley candle. I noticed it was low, but I got distracted, thinking about driving up to Jemez Pueblo to interview for a job I hope to get: teaching high school English on the reservation. Suddenly I heard a loud snap. My red Chimayo glass had cracked. Quickly, I blew out the flame and looked inside. The little metal wick holder rested against the glass and lines, like memory traces, spidered away from it, up the sides. Some of the red color had even burned away.

This upset me because, minutes before it happened, I had this thought: I don't have to change that candle now. Those glasses are made to take the heat. But nothing in this world is truly made to take the heat past a certain point. And then: crack. I know this very well because I have seen many things, many people, crack. I have cracked myself. But even knowing this, I didn't get up and change that candle. Instead, I looked away.

I waited until the red glass cooled and then I moved it carefully, hoping it wouldn't shatter. It didn't. I took it as a warning, a red light advising me to pay closer attention to important things. So at five this morning, I put in a new candle and cleared my mind for Shirley. After a quiet period, I remembered the day that I (determined to know everything about her) asked Shirley what her greatest pleasure was in life, and she immediately answered, "A job well done," and then added, "by me." That was before she took the Final Dive on a day in which she was sitting in her recliner in the kitchen, supervising me as I reorganized the food cupboard. Baking supplies, top shelf, right. (She almost never baked.) Canned vegetables, center. Cereals, left. "Have I got this pie crust in the right place, Shirley?" I asked, pretending to tremble. I made this (and other) cupboard-arrangement days into tense dramas, hammed it up as if I were terrified of her wrath. She was too weak to get up from her Mother's Day chair by then. She couldn't keep her house spotless, which was the way she liked it. So I "policed up," as Shirley put it: I vacuumed and raked her rugs even though I despise housework and almost never vacuum my own house, did the dishes several times a day, did not overload the washing machine or the dryer. I swatted flies and picked up their dead bodies with Kleenex, dusted her many collections, and watered her plants. I cleaned the refrigerator, warmed her tomato soup, and kept her many medications straight. I changed her morphine patches and cut up cantaloupes into tiny pieces with no green rind at the edges. I moved the TV into her bedroom and watched *The Bold and the Beautiful* with her. I made her tell me the whole sordid story of each character.

I know I did a good job.

A job, well done, by me.

But for some reason, in the back of my brain, I keep seeing the gold and white priest saying, "I can be a rotten person." And I keep hearing him say, "I ask you to forgive me."

I can make a list of all the good things I did for Shirley.

But I can't face this: it was late November. I had been there for six months. I was out of money. The part-time teaching job I had drummed up was about to end, and I didn't have anything else set up. I was afraid I would lose my teaching assistantship back in New Mexico, and I felt exhausted. And depressed. And helpless. I never expected Shirley to last so long.

I told Shirley, who looked like a corpse in her hospital bed, that I was going to leave in January.

I told her I was broke, which I was. Which I am.

She said, "Get me my checkbook. Let's figure out if we could both get by on my retirement." Under $1,000 a month.

I didn't want to tell her how I had borrowed money from several friends and maxed my credit cards.

I told her kids they needed to figure out how they were going to take care of her.

After I left. In January.

For a few weeks, Shirley said things like, "Of course, you have to get back to your life." And I would cry and say, "But I told you I was going to stay here until the last dog was hung." (Our euphemism.) And she would reply, "Julie, you have done so much, more than enough."

And then, finally, I let her sign her car over to me. To leave in.

And the very next day she took the Final Dive.

In my heart, I think she checked out before she was scheduled to go because she didn't want me to have to walk away from her on her deathbed.

Knowing this, and not knowing if I really would have gone, I feel like a rotten, rotten person.

But I don't know how or who to ask to be forgiven.

The Believers Center
Albuquerque, NM

This week I have been obsessing on Paul Timmons, the Catholic faith healer who came into Shirley's life during the last few months. Paul received the gift of healing hands when he was a travel agent on a visit to the church in Medjugorgje, Yugoslavia, where several children have seen the Virgin Mary. He now calls himself a charismatic. This term fascinates me, and when I study the Yellow Pages under "Churches," a frequent pastime of late, and find a whole section on charismatic churches, I decide to go to one. The first one, the Believers Center, has a detailed message on the phone machine, including directions and the time of the Sunday service.

I have images of a tiny storefront church in which oddballs twitch and speak in tongues, maybe while doing some spiritual version of St. Vitus' Dance, and on the way to the church, which is on the slopes of the East mountains far from my South Valley home, I actually prepare for the question, Are you a believer? I plan to say, "I need some more belief in my life," or "I'm certainly willing to become one."

I speed along the interstate, Route 40, listening to the "Train to Glory," a Sunday morning gospel show on KUNM radio. The music evokes pleasant images of Marvin Gaye—before his own father, the church minister, blew him to Kingdom Come with a shotgun. I exit at Tramway and head south to Central, the main drag through Albuquerque. I have never been this far east on Central and I look around with great interest, even though there's nothing to see except a housing development, dusty mountains, heavy truck traffic on I-40. The directions to the Believers Center are precise. I turn right onto Waterfalls Road and pull to the curb to try to figure out where I am in the numbers. Then I notice—a major shock—that the massive complex on my left *is* the Believers Center. The parking lot is bigger than the K-Mart mall where Shirley shopped, and already, forty-five minutes before the service, it is filling up. Men with ponytails and cowboy hats; preppies in button-down collars; women in jeans, fancy dresses, and business suits; children of every age, shape, size: they all head into the Believers Center. Families with many children and old couples holding hands stroll happily toward the door, fat prayer books in hand, as if believing is a magnet and they have no wish to resist.

At 9:23, I join the group, ready and willing to believe. A man opens the door for me and I step into an auditorium with stadium seating. Two video screens tower over the stage, and on them a sexy blonde belts out a rock and roll hymn. The stage itself is set up for a concert: grand piano, trap drums, five separate stand-up microphones. It reminds me of a time in L.A. when I was researching an article on stunt women, many of whom were Born Again Christians. I went with one, another sexy blonde, to Sunday church and there was a similar set up: rock band, a congregation of a thousand or more, a minister who wore Lucchesi boots and very tight pants.

In this Believers Center, a choir, dressed in black and white, three featured girl singers, and a male guitarist enter and the music begins. In front of me, a man who's obviously seen far more than his fair share of hard times lifts his hand into the air. "I am nothing without Christ" is written on his T-shirt in red letters that look like dripping blood. By the end of the first song, so many hands are waving around in the air that it looks like my T'ai-chi class. The words are projected onto the video screens, and the huge congregation, hundreds of people, sings along enthusiastically.

Finally, the blow-dried pastor, Marshall Townsley, comes forward and instructs us all to say, "Jesus is Lord!" I do not join in, but all around me people yell it, ad-libbing such cries as "Help me, Jesus!" and "That's the truth!" and "Amen!" A man directly behind me makes comments like this, loudly, all through the service, which lasts from 9:30 until 11:45. Over and over, he says "I am nothing without you, Lord." Meanwhile, a friendly black woman who sits to my left murmurs, "You got that right!" every few minutes.

The co-minister, the minister's wife, Cindi, takes the microphone and says something very close to this: "It's good to be back home. We spent the last week in a beautiful place with a lot of spiritually dead people." God had blessed her and her husband, she says, with a week in a time-share in Cancun, Mexico. I am shocked by her words. Shame on you, I think, which is not unlike what I said under my breath to Shirley's crack-pot funeral priest (in her Stage Two delirium, Shirley referred to him as "Father Go-Fish," which I found hilarious) when he started up against abortion during our last goodbye to my sister—the mother of six. I barely listen as this preacher-woman continues, and tune her out completely after she warns us that "The promises of God are not microwaveable."

Honestly, here on my sixth Sunday, I am feeling that church is a closed society, no matter how many "Welcome!" signs are put up outside, no matter how much hand-holding there is, no matter how enthusiastically they say, "Let's all turn around and greet our neighbor!" It's ironic to me that I'm even in church, doing homage to Shirley, when Shirley herself stopped church-going long before she got sick. Still, she considered herself on the square with her God, and she had spiritual confidence and peace. At least she did up until the last three months. Until Paul Timmons, the Catholic charismatic, came into her life. Then she began to doubt her relationship with God. She began to think about getting back into the Catholic church, and she was more scared. She had been so confident before: refusing chemotherapy; calmly saying, "It's not like I'm a young person. I've had my life"; wanting to be left alone. But post-Paul, she questioned her motives. "I don't want to go back to the church because I'm in a jam," she said, sweeping her hand across the hospital bed. She wondered if God was mad at her for leaving the church. She changed from being amazingly serene to doubtful. Maybe that happens when a person approaches Death's Door, but in my mind, I associate her discomfort with Paul. I can't help it.

Marshall Townsley preaches about the four kinds of grace: convicting, quickening, living, and dying. He calls dying grace the bridge that makes it possible to leave one's family and loved ones and go to God. I think about Shirley during her last three months—the good weeks after the healing and the bad ones after the crash. During those months, I revised my definition of grace, which had previously leaned toward the Hemingway grace-under-pressure model. Innocently, I had thought that grace was something you exhibited, something you *did,* through an exercise of will and/or moral choice. But watching Shirley, I learned that what you do, especially when you're dying, only reflects what's already inside of you. You simply cannot have grace under pressure unless you have grace inside of you already.

The highlight is Pastor Townsley's dramatization of convicting grace—the grace that occurs when you finally accept Jesus. He asks a white-haired man to come up front, and then he selects three other men to act as devils intent on keeping this would-be convertee back from Jesus. He instructs these devils to hold the man by the neck and arms and to stand in front of him to block his way. When the man receives convicting grace—illustrated by the preacher, who merely extends his hand to the beleaguered one—he can break free and step out of the devils' clutches. The crowd roars when he does so. The minister says that the devils will cower now, and sure enough, when the saved man heads back across the stage, they shrink back and cover their faces.

The crowd hollers, and people stamp their feet.

"I want to go to God," Shirley whispered over and over again in Stage Two of the Final Dive. And then, her voice mystified, she added, "Why doesn't God want me? I have to burn more." We stood around her bed, panic stricken. Pastor Townsley has said that "death's sting has been removed for the believer." He is dead wrong about this. Death's sting was not removed for my sister. A believer if there ever was one.

Five new people receive the spirit, including a young boy from my row who fidgeted during the whole service and seemed to smirk as he raised his hand; then the minister warns those of us in the audience who have not taken Jesus into our hearts that we may not partake of communion. "Don't do it!" he advises. If we do, it will lead to our destruction, he says. I pass the tray of bread and tiny cups of wine on to the man next to me with an Attila-the-Hun hairdo, dyed blonde.

Thursday

I wake up actually gnashing my teeth at 4:23 in the morning. The covers are in such a tangle that I can't even stretch out my legs. It really enrages me that pastors and priests set up an "us vs. them" scenario over the simple act of taking communion. At Shirley's funeral, Father Go-Fish said, "Good People, communion is just for Catholics. If you are not a Catholic, or if you are one and have not made your Easter Duty, or are living in sin, you cannot take communion today." I don't understand how they can think in this way. Communion with God should be for everybody.

I get up, light my Shirley candle, sit on the bed, and stew.

My search for the spirit (and Shirley) is, by turns, riling me up, relegating me to observer status, and taking me nowhere in the vicinity of understanding. "What did you expect?" I growl into the candlelight. "That you'd just jump on the bandwagon?" Even Shirley did not do that—with death leering down on her. At first, she resisted Catholicism. When our mother, determined to save her soul, sent a priest and a nun over, Shirley politely sent them packing. But then Paul Timmons emerged out of nowhere, and Shirley changed. She got better, and then she got worse.

I get up, find my glasses, open the dictionary, and look up the word "charismatic."

> Charismatic: n. 1. a member of a charismatic group or movement. 2. a person who supposedly has some divinely inspired power, as the ability to prophesy.
>
> Charisma: 1. in Christian theology, a divinely inspired gift, grace, or talent, as for prophesying, healing, etc. 2. a special quality of leadership that captures the popular imagination and inspires unswerving allegiance and devotion.
>
> Charismatic: a. 1. pertaining to charisma. 2. designating or of any various religious groups or movements that stress direct divine inspiration, manifested as in glossolalia, healing powers, etc.

Glossolalia: n. an ecstatic or apparently ecstatic utterance of unintelligible speechlike sounds, viewed by some as a manifestation of deep religious experience.

Even the dictionary, the theoretically objective source, uses the word "supposedly" as in "supposedly has some divinely inspired power." But Paul Timmons, Shirley's personal charismatic, healed a woman (ironically, also named Carter) who is the mother of a friend of my younger sister, Laurie. She had lung cancer, he laid hands on her, and it disappeared. This is why we contacted Paul in the first place, way back in August. He made an appointment to pray for and with Shirley over the phone a few days later. I called all Shirley's kids, our sisters, our parents, her friends, her co-workers. I asked them all to join in this prayer session, wherever they were.

This was one hot summer night when we thought Shirley would die any second. We gathered in her living room: Shirley, her younger daughter Kim, and Kim's two-year-old daughter, Melanie, my sister Laurie, Shirley's buddy Marcia, and me. We sat together in a circle, holding hands, while Shirley prayed with Paul on the phone. Kim, as instructed by Paul, placed her hands on either side of Shirley's emaciated, jaundiced body. Little Melanie sat in my lap, looking curiously from one of us to the next. At age two, she never even peeped.

A few hundred miles away, Shirley's eldest, Billy, his wife, Marlous, and their sons, Andrew and Alan, sat together in their living room and looked at family pictures of themselves and Shirley.

Julie, exploring a cave in the West with her friend Bill, stopped and listened.

Johnny sat alone in his house near Boston.

Jimmy found a quiet corner at work and was silent.

Neal prayed in his apartment.

Our parents and our sister, Joanie, who was visiting, prayed at their house; the parents in the TV room and Joanie on the front porch.

Our sister Mary, in California, clutched her crucifix and begged God to save Shirley.

Our sister Janet, in western Canada, lit candles. Cried. Held onto Shirley's last gift (an antique hair receiver—a box in which ladies of yesteryear stuffed their hair after cleaning it out of their brushes, though why I don't know).

Two of Laurie's children said the rosary in their living room.

At the nursing home where Shirley had worked, several of the aides gathered together, held hands, and prayed.

In Holland, Marlous' mother stayed up late (because of the time difference) and held a photo of Shirley, held Shirley in her heart.

Everybody, everywhere prayed to God to spare Shirley. We could not let her go. We could not bear it.

When it was over, when Shirley hung up, she was crying. We all were. "I'll never doubt the power of love again," she said, and then she stood up and walked outside for the first time in weeks. It was sunset. Beautiful colors streaked across the sky. I stood in the driveway and watched her float across the grass in her nightgown, like an angel.

Or a ghost.

Paul promised to make a special trip from Georgia to see Shirley in person in September. We could not imagine that she would make it that long, but she did. He instructed us to meet him in the parking lot of Notre Dame Church in Malone.

"How will I know you?" Shirley asked.

"I have very black hair," he replied.

"I have very yellow skin," Shirley said, and they both laughed merrily.

The night before his arrival, my sister Mary, who had come for what we referred to as "the healing," overheard this conversation between our parents:

> Ma: Johnny, I really think we should make a contribution
> to Paul.
> Dad: Well, what do you think we should give him?
> Ma: I think...well...I think maybe five dollars.
> Dad: The guy's coming all the way from Georgia. (Pause)
> Give him ten.

We collected money and put it into an envelope.

The next morning, we gathered in the parking lot of the church. Julie drove Shirley, who needed a wheelchair and a bucket to throw up into. All of Shirley's kids were there, their spouses and lovers and children;

our parents; four of Shirley's five sisters; two aunts; Marcia; several other friends.

Paul arrived with his fiancée in a sports utility vehicle. When I saw him, I thought of Johnny Cash in his I'm-the-man-in-black phase. (My sister Janet, who met him later, thought he looked like an Elvis impersonator.) No one at the church knew we were coming, and a robed priest said we couldn't go inside because a funeral was scheduled at eleven—this was 10:30—and mourners were already present, but Paul led us around to a side chapel called the "Crying Room," and we stormed in. As Paul instructed, we formed a circle around Shirley. Later, my sister Mary felt compelled to write out her memories of Shirley's life. She called this biography "Dear Lady" because, as Mary put it, "In my lifetime, Shirley has always been the holiest, best woman I had ever known and I thought she was about as near to the Blessed Mother as you could get." Mary sent her piece to Shirley by FedEx, and it arrived just before the Final Dive. I read it to Shirley, a little each night. We finished it just before she slipped into Stage Two, when she really couldn't have listened anymore.

This is the way Mary described the healing service for her "Dear Lady":

> We all went inside. I can't begin to tell you the feeling that permeated that room. We all formed a wide circle around Shirley's wheelchair. Paul, dressed totally in black, knelt down on one knee just to Shirley's left. I was standing behind them with my sister Julie on my left and my mother on my right. I could look directly into Paul's face.
>
> He has benevolent eyes and beautiful hands, large hands. He said the most beautiful prayers. He began by saying to Shirley, "Now Shirley, this is very important. You must try to concentrate as hard as you can. If Jesus were right here in this room with us and he said to you, 'You can ask for anything you want, anything at all and it will be given to you,' what would you ask for?"
>
> Shirley said softly, "I would ask for health and long life for my entire family."
>
> "And what else?" Paul pressed.
>
> "I would ask to be cured of my cancer."

"And is there anything else?" Paul asked.

"I'd ask that my father's knees be less painful and my mother would always be able to see."

"All right," Paul said, "Now I'm going to place my hands on you where you experience the pain," and kneeling on one knee, he placed one hand on her abdomen and one on her back and he began to pray. I can't remember everything he said, but I heard him say clearly that he wasn't asking that Shirley's cancer go into remission, or be partially cured; he was asking that it be eradicated. He prayed, too, that if it was not God's will that she be healed, and if it was Shirley's time to die, that the Blessed Mother would take her by the hand and lead her straight into heaven.

"Dear Lady," he said that morning, "we cannot forget about you. You are the mother of our God."

I heard those words as he spoke them and they have stayed in my mind, whispering themselves over and over ever since. We said the Our Father, the Hail Mary, and the Glory Be to the Father together and he asked Shirley if she was experiencing less pain. She asked if she could get up and walk around.

As she began to walk around, we all stood silently watching and hoping that the pain which had been her constant companion for nine months was gone. She seemed uncertain but slowly she said, "It seems incredible, really, but I think it may be gone."

Paul said, "Come and sit down again." He placed his hands on her again. This time he prayed in thanksgiving for the healing which he hoped had taken place. His hands were very warm and when his hands were warm, he thought it was a positive sign. We were all crying now, tears of relief and joy and hope all mixed in together. When his prayers were over, Paul said to Shirley, "Don't go home and mow the lawn."

Of course, we laughed but I will never forget the look in his eyes. He said to Shirley, "You have my 1-800 number. Call me day or night." As Shirley got up to the hugs of everyone in her family, Paul slipped out of the church.

That day, after the healing, I ran after Paul and found him in the parking lot. I tried to give him the envelope full of money, but he flatly, adamantly, refused it. "Maybe I could make a donation to the Center for Peace," I said. This is his organization. "If you send it, I'll send it right back," he answered. "Well," I stuttered, "if you ever have need of a writer, call me." I couldn't think of anything else to say. He and his girlfriend climbed into the Jeep and drove away. I ran back inside the Crying Room, where everyone was crying.

Slowly, I return to the present, to my *casita*, very aware of an oppressive heaviness on my lap. I glance down to see it's my massive dictionary, still turned to "G," where I have looked up glossolalia. For no reason, my eye catches on this word:

Glory hole: 1. an opening in a furnace, showing the light within. 2. a place, as a drawer, closet, etc., where things are heaped together untidily (Coloq.)

On Sundays, I realize, I am peering directly into the Glory Hole, looking for the light. But it's a mess in there.

It's a real mess.

St. John Bosco Roman Catholic Church
Malone, NY

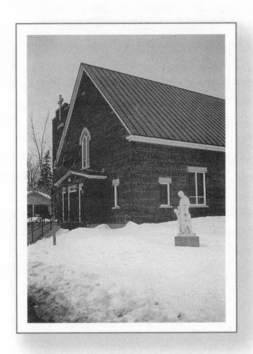

I go to the North Country for spring break, back east to see my husband, my parents and sisters, nieces and nephews, dog and kitty-cat. I am so exhausted that I fall asleep before the plane even leaves the runway and don't wake up until we land in Albany, New York, where Robert is waiting. We drive north, four more hours, to where the plow piles of snow on either side of the road are higher than the car windows. I am coming back to Shirley's world for the first time since she died. When I left here in January, I was shocked at how disorienting it was to touch down in a Shirley-less landscape. I wandered aimlessly around the UNM campus looking for a way back into my ex-life. Many, many people inquired after my sister. "She died on Christmas night," I said, over and over, like an actress in a play by Samuel Beckett.

Before we go home to Owl's Head, we drive into Malone so I can look at churches. There are two possibilities for tomorrow morning, both Roman Catholic in honor of Shirley. I will not go to her funeral church in a nearby town because I still have an extremely bad attitude toward the priest who made every possible mistake during her funeral. That leaves Notre Dame, where we met Paul on September 17th, or St. John Bosco, where the resident priest is Father Tom, the priest who came to hear Shirley's last confession, sent to her by Paul. This confession, for which I left the house, lasted five minutes. I stayed away for three hours, assuming it would take that long. "Maybe for you," my sister laughed. She described it, right afterward, as the easiest five minutes of her life.

We turn left off Main Street at the courthouse, pass the hot dog factory and continue down into the part of Malone my mother calls the Depot. My mother grew up five miles from here on a farm. My father was the physical education teacher in her high school. On their sixtieth wedding anniversary, my mother told me that when she saw him for the first time, she thought, He has a nice set of shoulders. Too bad he's so short.

When I see the church, I suddenly remember that the locals call it St. John the Bosco. As a kid, visiting in the summers, I wondered if "the Bosco" was similar to "the Baptist." Perhaps, I thought, St. John was the inventor of Bosco, the chocolate syrup, raised to sainthood by some Italian pope with a sweet tooth. As a teenager, I was once part of a group of kids who placed a large bottle of Bosco in the hands of the statue in front of the church in the middle of the night. It all comes back as we inch our way down the icy street toward a sign announcing mass at ten.

From there, we proceed to Notre Dame. The church is closed down and boarded up.

So, in the morning, I head to St. John the Bosco. As always, it is snowing as I ease down the mountain into Malone in Shirley's Ford Escort, which she signed over to me the night before she took the Final Dive. She had told Mary Lou, our Hospice nurse, that I wouldn't accept it, making it an item of unfinished business that kept her here on earth. Our sister Janet, a palliative care nurse, had told me this two months before, but I couldn't bear to take the car then, even knowing that Shirley wanted to give it to me when the last dog was hung. But that Sunday night in December, I found the paperwork and Shirley signed the Escort over to me in tiny, shaky handwriting. "I had to foist it on you," she said, and then she laughed, her teeth huge, like a skeleton's. I called Kim, who had been with her mother for two weeks, into the bedroom to take our picture at this precise moment. I am holding my sister's hand so tightly that you can't even see it in the photo.

The very next morning, Shirley could not get up.

That morning, I called from my part-time teaching job, and Kim was sobbing. "Mom's so much weaker," she cried. "She got so much weaker overnight." My own knees went weak, and I heard blood throbbing in my ears. Kim had to leave. She was long overdue at her job in Vermont, and it was her only daughter's third birthday. She is a calm person, but now she was beside herself. It seared her heart to watch her mother edge away. She could not bear to leave Shirley alone until I could get there, so she called Marcia. Marcia came, and Kim left, in agony. She never saw her mother alive again.

I finished school that day and drove to Shirley's. A strange drive: knowing Shirley had truly entered the departure lounge; knowing that the time was upon her (and me); driving in the car she'd just officially given up; turning on the radio; hearing Iz K sing "Somewhere over the Rainbow." It was like being thirty feet underwater with a limited supply of oxygen.

That evening, I placed the commode right next to the bed and helped Shirley onto it. When I lifted her back to the edge of her hospital bed, I let go of her to straighten the covers and she fell backward— WHOMP—and cracked her head on the metal rails. "Shirley!" I screamed, shocked that a human body, Shirley's body, could flop backward so fast. "It didn't hurt," she said as her eyes teared up. I lifted her up, shifted her onto her pillow, and covered her. "That's it. I'm never getting out of bed again," she announced, quietly. And then she added, "And I'm not eating anymore either." I never asked her to, not once.

Within days, all she wanted was fresh water and God anyway.

Later, the Hospice people told me that allowing a person not to eat is the single most difficult thing for most families. For me, it was easy. I don't know why. I'm afraid to know why.

The Catholics heading into St. John the Bosco are dressed for the North Country—heavy jackets, boots, scarves, mittens, more. The faces are light green, the winter pallor that drains out the color, starting in

November. Everyone looks numb. Numb happens, I think as I study them, after prolonged deprivation of something vitally important.

I felt numb when I heard Shirley was sick. I had no feeling left because, though I can barely admit it to myself, I had felt seriously deprived of Shirley for many years. I turn up the heater and dig my fingernails into the ice that is forming on the side window. It leaves little trails, like memory traces, but I do not follow them into that Shirley-less period that lasted almost a decade. Rather, I see myself picking up the phone last March and dialing Shirley's number. I was standing up because I was too nervous to sit down. When she answered, I said, "Is this the person to whom I am speaking?", the old Lily Tomlin joke I always used on Shirley. Quickly, I followed up with, "Hey, what's this I hear about you being sick?"

"It's true," she said. "The doctors can't find out what's wrong with me."

I grilled her about her symptoms and promised to visit on my break from school in May. Then, at the end of our conversation, I took a big breath. I wanted to say something, but my lips could barely shape such foreign words. Then I said, "Keep me posted, O.K. Shirley? Because I'm one of the people who cares about you."

"I'll see you when you come in May," she responded. "Don't worry."

When I tried to hang up, I dropped the receiver and then knocked the phone off the table. It split off its metal bottom—cracked open, like I was. I flopped on the couch. I felt sick myself. "Why was it so hard to tell her you care?" Julie Reichert asked, but I shook my head. "I cannot even begin to explain it," I said. But in my heart, I knew I could. Just not then. "Just not now," I say out loud as I open the car door.

The church is red brick with lovely old wooden doors, which I enter with a sense of familiarity. This is the Roman Catholic church of my childhood. Honestly, it's the church that turned me against religion. Too many rules. Too shameful a history. Too much guilt. Too many ways to burn. When I sit down, the first thing I see is the wooden confessional with "Father Tom" carved over the door. This startles me, sends me reeling back to the day he met my sister. When she was on her deathbed.

Suddenly, a voice booms over the loudspeaker and down the center aisle march three men in dingy vestments and a woman who holds a sacred book high above her head. This surprises me. When I was a Catholic, there were no females in sight anywhere during mass. We had nuns with yardsticks for smacking your hands instead. I scoot across the seat and ask a young wife which man is Father Tom.

"The one with the grey hair," she whispers. I nod and thank her.

All three of these men have grey hair, two priests and an altar man. (Shirley's funeral mass was also served by an altar man, a Mohawk from the Akwasasne reservation who had been Shirley's sons' Boy Scout leader. All summer, he brought fresh tomatoes from his garden when tomatoes were the only thing Shirley could stand to eat.) I don't ask this woman for further clarification, though. I just follow along, amazed that my memory is supplying the words to prayers I have not said in over thirty years. And supplying them in both Latin and English. I do not say them out loud, though, because rote responses scare me, especially when I'm the one making them.

The priest sings the mass, but I don't listen because I'm fixated on the second priest, the quiet one who sits off to the side. He wears a hooded robe and sandals with heavy socks, and has white hair and a white beard that form a ring, like a tiny mane, around his face. Soon, during the sermon, the priest introduces himself as an out-of-towner, and I learn that the man I can't take my eyes off is Father Tom. Maybe I'm a sucker for a robe and sandals, but I think he looks like a truly kind man, the kind of priest who can make a dying person's last confession, the first in thirty years, the easiest five minutes of her life. I openly stare at him, as in the background the visiting priest cheerleads for a spiritual retreat that begins here tomorrow night in which participants will learn more about fasting, listening, and abstinence—though from what, he doesn't mention.

I glance around at the parishioners and wonder how many will brave the sub-zero weather, the snow, and the ice to come to church three more times this week. I know I won't. I feel sorry, in a way, for the priest. Excitement does not light the eyes of the congregation. On the other hand, nearly every person goes to communion.

At the end, Father Tom stands in the rear door to greet each person. As I wait my turn, I hope for a moment of communion myself: some kind of electrical current, a charge, from his fingertips, perhaps lasers from his eyes. But instead, it's just a cool hand, a distracted glance, a blast of freezing air as I step out the door.

Friday

I go to Shirley's house. It is odd to drive down her dirt road, deep with mud. There is much less snow here, maybe five or six inches as opposed to several feet at my own place in the mountains. There is no ice on her roof, unlike at mine, where icicles stretch like winter prison bars all the way to the ground. I park in Shirley's driveway expecting to be swamped by memories, but nothing happens.

Shirley never locked her house, ever, in all the years she lived in it, but now it is locked up and I have no key. I like to think symbolically, so I imagine the house is where Shirley is and the door is Death's Door, locked to me, for now. I can only speculate about what's going on inside. And, of course, I wonder if she can see me out here (down here), and if she is intact in some mysterious way, and happy.

The house looks stark, but that is normal in the winter when the trees are bare and the flowers are gone. Until a few years ago, it was shingled dark green. It had little holes all over it where insulation had been blown in and the circular plugs had dropped out and vanished. Then Shirley's son Johnny, the wild man of the family, gave her money to remodel, and she installed a forest green tin roof, white siding, and all new windows. But she barely got to live in it when it was done.

I must have come here a million times in my hippie and New York years. I came with VW bus loads of hippies, with musician, artist, and actor boyfriends, with women buddies who did such things as join up with a passing carnival. Once, I brought a contortionist home from the Franklin County Fair, and Shirley and the kids set up chairs in the kitchen and watched him put a nail up his nose, roll his eyeballs like two spinning tops, and pull his stomach in until he was only four inches thick.

I came here from downstate, from Boston, Miami, Montréal, New York, L.A., and New Mexico. I came single, married, annulled, and married again. I have come here rail thin and tubby, broke and financially fit, depressed and feeling happy. And no matter what, I would talk and talk and talk, and Shirley would listen, deeply, usually while she was stripping paint off old antiques or staining them or sewing. She took old junk and transformed it. She loved to fix things that were broken. Old things came alive in her hands. And so did people.

When her symptoms first started and I was researching them on the Internet, I returned again and again to web pages on pancreatic cancer. This was because when Shirley had a C.T. scan, a "shadow" appeared on the pancreas. The incompetent radiologist and gastrointerologist agreed that it was nothing to worry about, and treatment for ulcers began. But the first time I went to the web and read that exposure to solvents was considered a prime cause of cancer of the pancreas, right then, I knew.

I am sitting in the dining room of my little house in the North Country, and these are the things in my visual field that Shirley refinished for me, using solvents: the wainscoting in the kitchen, the kitchen floor, the china cabinet, the dining room table, two other tables, and a mirror. And that's just my house, this room. Shirley's gifts fill a dozen houses. And her own.

For years, her house was a repair shop, with old furniture, whole and in pieces, piled everywhere. When her daughters visited, they had to clear a narrow path through the stacks of antiques to their beds. There were always projects going on in the kitchen, the laundry room, the sun porch. Paint brushes soaked in solvents on the kitchen counter. Shirley never wore gloves. Well, no one did when she started to refinish antiques forty years ago.

When Shirley got her diagnosis, when her children flocked to her in disbelief, she was very stoic. "If it's my time, I'm ready to go," she said. Then once she added wistfully, "But there were so many things I wanted to do."

"What, Mom?" Julie cried. "What?"

"Well..." Shirley paused. "I really wanted to clean out that sun porch."

Everyone howled, but the next day, her kids and our sister Janet had a work bee. They lugged the old furniture—it would never be refinished now—to the barn. They wallpapered, put up a white ceiling, put down a rug. They made the sun porch beautiful like she would have, completely transforming it in two days. Shirley sat there on the daybed every day afterward and looked out the windows at the flowers. I could see her there as I sat in her driveway, staring into her house just as she had stared out of it. Motionless.

Tomorrow, I return to Albuquerque.

Where I have not one piece of furniture that Shirley refinished for me.

Just before I leave New York, my younger sister Laurie tells me about a dream she has had: some spirit form of Shirley and Laurie and I are all together in Shirley's house. Shirley is walking around picking up various things and studying them. "Isn't this beautiful," she says as she looks at each one. "Isn't this nice?" We follow her. After a while, she turns and says to Laurie, "You and Julie should stop crying now."

The First United Methodist Church
Albuquerque, NM

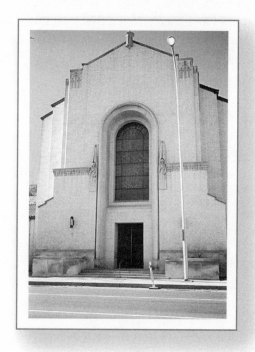

For the first time in two months, I consider skipping church. The novelty has worn off, and no one even asks me anymore on Mondays where I went to church the day before and what happened. I am all alone in this. Like a gambler irrationally expecting to hit the jackpot, I show up every week in my best outfit, maintain the rhythm, do the dance. My friend Julie Shigekuni has explained to me that the churches are a meditation: "It makes no difference what you use—a sound, a candle, a mantra. It's what happens when you're there that counts," she said. But often, I find myself longing for what doesn't happen. I want God, but I'll settle for a sudden rush of belonging or even a strong desire to return to one of these churches. This doesn't occur. However, I feel stabilized by my Sunday practice. It gives my grief a shape and form which I can, and need to, look at calmly.

I get up and drive to the First United Methodist Church, arriving there fewer than seven hours after I have landed back in Albuquerque. Above the inner entry door is a notation: "Nineteen centuries have come and gone and today He is the central figure of the human race—Jesus Christ." It concludes a narrative by Sharon Higgins which begins, "He was born in an obscure village...worked in a carpenter shop until he was thirty...became an itinerant preacher...never had an office, a family, or a house...didn't go to college," etc. I like the storytelling, but I do not believe for a New York minute that Christ is the central figure of the human race.

Even when Shirley was dying and began to pray out loud to Jesus, when I would hear her say that name, I became impatient and inwardly aggressive. I tried to transform or at least stuff my negative feelings, but I couldn't. "Oh no," I muttered to myself as Shirley prayed, "here we go again with Jay-zus." To me, Christ equals Catholicism—the religion in which you're born guilty, your soul black with the Original Sin you didn't even commit; the religion in which God the Father watches you constantly, waiting for you to screw up so he can throw you into hell to burn for all eternity.

I accept that Christ is not my savior, and enter this enormous church. Aside from three senior citizens and me, there is no one here, though, oddly, stuffed animals lounge at the end of every pew. Pastel dogs with floppy ears, smiling tigers with long whiskers, and fat teddy bears with buttons for eyes are present today to listen to God's word. But then, a side door opens and a small crowd rushes in, including the musicians: a pony-tailed guitarist, a pianist, a flutist, a synthesizer-player, and twelve singers.

The minister, Dr. Terry Anderson, is lanky and wears a western-cut suit. Like most of the congregation, he is elderly. The service begins with several hymns, sung with gusto by the Fourth Street Sound. In the last one, "I'll Fly Away," the singers clap in unison and it hits me that if I squint my eyes, it looks like they are doing the "bluebirds fly" segment of the dance we created to "Somewhere over the Rainbow" in Shirley's living room during the Final Dive. A whole flock of bluebirds is flying in the Methodist church today. I keep my eyes squinty for the duration.

In this blur, I remember the moment from my hippie days when I dramatically selected a reading for my own funeral. It was called "I Am

Flying Home," a meditation by Swami Paramahansa Yogananda. Of course, I changed the words a little. Not being a fan of the patriarchy (then or now), I could not imagine saying I was flying home to "the Father." Fathers clip your wings. They cage you up, lock you in, and make you doubt your ability to sing. You fly away from, not toward, them as far and as fast as your wings can carry you. Or at least I did. I stayed away a long, long time. For years and years, my only connection to the family I was born into was Shirley. Without her, nothing.

"Don't fly away!" Reverend Anderson laughs when the singing stops. "Don't fly away before we have the chance to greet each other!" And the whole place erupts. People spill out of their pews and singers flood down the center aisle. Everyone is shaking hands and saying "Good morning." I make a 360-degree circle, greeting everyone around me. But I'm still thinking about flying, away and toward, remembering how, near the end, Marcia instructed me to open the window when Shirley passed so her spirit could fly away. Could it be real, this idea that we fly off to a better place when we die?

The night Shirley died, around 1:30 in the morning, I called Marcia. She had been listening to Glenn Gould, whose music had carried her far away, far above the earth, so far away she had become scared. As Shirley got worse and worse, Marcia often whispered to her that when her time came, she, Marcia, would go as far as she could with her. But that night, as Marcia felt herself flying away, she became frightened and rushed back to her bedroom, where the phone rang, and I gave her the sad news. Marcia immediately dressed and ran out into the snow. She looked up into the black sky at the Star Path, wondering how far she had gone with Shirley. She stayed out there in the sub-zero cold until some form of wildlife—an owl, she thinks—swooped in too close and she ran back inside.

Reverend Anderson's sermon is on "That Nasty Word: Repent!" From a Bible passage (Luke 13: 1-9), he extrapolates that repentance is actually a joyful thing because repentance creates a clean slate every time. I have always wondered about clean slates, forgiveness, and freedom, but ever since the Greek Orthodox priest, I think about it even more. Two days after that Sunday, a student of mine came to my office to tell me that she felt I had unnecessarily embarrassed her in class. I explained why I had done what I did, which I felt was justified. She's a nice kid, though, and I spontaneously added a quick apology for hurting her feelings. "Will you forgive me?" I asked as an experiment. "I forgave you right away," she answered. But I noticed that she still felt a need to confront me.

Shirley was excellent at forgiveness. If she's watching, is she forgiving me for trying to put her life and death into words? For turning my sadness, all our sadness, into a Sunday-by-Sunday account? Shirley kept secrets, and I tell them. I know I am trying in some way to clean my slate so I can start again, but there's so much to erase, so many mistakes, and the biggest one of all was, "I'm leaving in January."

I miss my sister terribly as the service ends, maybe because I've just returned from the North Country, and she wasn't there. She wasn't at Sunday dinner. She is gone, gone, gone. And I want her back.

When Shirley was in Stage Three and her daughter Julie was talking to her one night—perhaps a day or two before Shirley died—I heard my niece whisper, "You don't have to come back here, Mom. You don't." She was quiet for a while and then added, "But if you do…find me."

Friday

Yesterday I got up and lit my Shirley candle. I did the Five Tibetan Rites and then returned to bed, in the almost-dark, to drink my morning coffee and watch the daylight roll in. I called Robert, back in New York where two more feet of snow had fallen, read a book for a good while, and left my *casita* at 9:30 to go visit Julie Shigekuni and Issa. Issa has grown by fifty percent—having put on just over three pounds. She looks like a mature infant now, if such a thing is possible. Then I went to the Albuquerque Public Library to do some research, then taught my English 101 class, and, afterward, flopped on the couch in the office of another graduate student, Logan. We talked about Paris, where she wants to live. She has just made her first trip there. She had to wait a long time for it—until her daughters were grown up and gone. Myself, I went when I was young, and haven't been back since.

I arrived home at 6:30.

And my Shirley candle was still burning.

I was shocked because my pattern is—has always been, ever since I lit it the first time—to blow out the candle as a way of closing off the Shirley part of the day. I like to keep this time separate, fenced off like a very private garden. That little halo of light flickering in the red glass accuses me of betraying my sister. Of forgetting her. I stand over the candle, staring into the flame. Has Shirley slipped permanently out of my life because I left this important psychic gate open by mistake? Maybe she's slipped *into* my life, out of the isolation I imposed on her spirit in my five-in-the-morning ritual. Or maybe it's just nothing.

Today, I asked Julie Shigekuni if she believes that the universe is organized in such a way that every person gets exactly what she or he needs in order to evolve. I notice that, for me, it seems harder to let this idea go than it was to let my sister go, at least at the end.

"I think what's important is doing things in the right sequence in the moment," says Julie as she sautés Portobello mushrooms over a low flame. "Right now, I want to put the ingredients in at precisely the right time, in the right order." She stirs some more. "To make a good frittata."

I hold Issa while she cooks. I have hooked my neck onto the back of the chair and created a forty-five degree slope with my body on which Issa sleeps in her little yellow jumpsuit. Julie's green parakeet sits on my shoulder.

"So you don't think it's organized," I persist, wanting clarity.

"I think that's beyond the scope of my understanding," she says. "It's not something I expect to know in my lifetime." I admire Julie—her willingness to live in the mystery and master the moment, which is everything.

Hidden Mountain Zen Center
Albuquerque, NM

My car has broken down twice in the past two days. The first time, I got it going by adding fuel injector cleaner to the gas and letting it sit overnight in the UNM parking lot, but last night, it simply refused to start. This is the 1987 Saab that my friend Michele gave me when I returned to New Mexico. In that one month, I was given two cars, but Shirley's Escort is in New York (the weather was too bad to drive it home); the Saab is parked off Central, and I am sitting in a bright red Budget Rent-a-Car in front of the Hidden Mountain Zen Center at nine on this Sunday morning.

The zen center is a two-story building, wooden with peeling paint, in a quiet neighborhood close to downtown Albuquerque. In a pie-shaped park across the street, three homeless men wearing dirty jackets and knit hats sit on picnic tables and smoke. A huge squawking black crow overhead weighs down the flimsy branch of a cottonwood tree.

I have only been to one zen meditation in my life, and that was fifteen years ago. I found it excruciating to sit still, and I left early—drove home to Venice Beach and took a swim in the Santa Monica Bay, which for me was a more fruitful meditation. I have no idea how I will fare today.

I leave my shoes on the rack on the porch and go in, but a young woman hustles me back out and explains in whispers that the members of this zendo are participating in a silent retreat this weekend. She takes me upstairs where there is personal instruction for newcomers. After that, I will join in the sitting meditation, which is already in progress.

We go to a small room where a grey-haired white man and a grey-haired white woman give us newcomers tips on how to sit (using a cushion, a stool, or a chair), how to hold our backs, heads, fingers, and eyes, how to press our knees into the floor, and how to breathe. We are told to notice and acknowledge our thoughts, but to let them go. We should count our breaths, one to ten, starting over if we get distracted by a passing thought. During all the time that follows, I never make it past one.

"What if something hurts?" I ask, because my back already aches to the right of my spine in the place I injured it thirty years ago while stacking wicker furniture outside a store in Cambridge, Mass, in my hippie days. Every single day on that job, I lugged fifty pieces of wicker furniture out to the sidewalk at nine and lugged them back inside at five forty-five.

"Just become the pain," says my teacher. Both he and the woman wear robes—many layers of black—and some kind of embroidered, black-on-black bag around their necks. Moments later, when we rise to join the group downstairs, I notice with alarm that they can hardly get up. Their knees are shot, like my father's are.

("I spent too many years demonstrating descents off the flying rings," he has often told me. As a consequence, he now lives in a reclining chair. This past week, he turned ninety-four. "How are you doing on your birthday?" I asked when I made my mandatory birthday call. "I read the obituary page and I wasn't on it. That's a good sign," he answered).

We go downstairs where thirty people silently march the perimeter of an empty room which has shiny wood floors, white walls, and white blinds. When the walkers return to their mats for further sitting, we join in for a thirty-minute session. I fail miserably, which is no big surprise to me. I repeatedly yawn, which causes tears to roll down my face. I brush them away, even knowing that I'm not supposed to move.

Sometimes I peek at the other meditators, all of whom sit perfectly still, or I close my eyes instead of keeping them open but cast downward as I've been instructed. I try, between countings to one breath, to focus on the connection between all beings in the universe, or at least on my breath, but I end up worrying about how I will get the Saab to the garage. How I will pay for the repairs.

The half hour goes fast, and then we all move into the main room for the dharma talk. The Sensei, amid pomp and circumstance, settles on a pillow. Water is placed by his side, and one helper carries a small table and places it in front of him. Another man delivers a mystery package, wrapped in a black and white cloth. The Sensei spreads the cloth, which is purple inside, on the table to reveal the sacred book. Religion as we know it, I have decided, simply could not survive in a non-print culture.

His topic, like Pastor Townsley at the Believers Center, is devils and demons. These, he says, reading from the book, can be defined as mental blocks which prevent us from true understanding. These include seeking enlightenment for the benefit of oneself only, trying to rush enlightenment, glorifying a teacher, rejecting a teaching because of the personal behavior of the teacher, surrendering to passion, and rejecting passion. He repeatedly advises us to expect "endless effort, no gain" in our battle against these devils. We all sit on our pillows and listen attentively. Incense burns before a statue of Buddha on a small altar.

When the dharma talk ends, we form two lines, our backs against opposing walls, while various people (all men) carry incense and objects I don't recognize back and forth before us. Frequently, we bow. Most people bow so low they touch the floor with their foreheads, though this is not required. My personal trainer, the man from upstairs, folds a piece of material into a precise pattern on a pillow, and walks around it many times. I have no clue what he's doing. Then we chant for a bit and wrap it all up with a rousing rendition of the dharma rules, which vibrate throughout the room:

> Sentient beings are numberless; I vow to save them.
> Attachments are inexhaustible; I vow to put an end to
>   them.
> Dharmas are boundless; I vow to master them.
> The Buddha way is unsurpassable; I vow to attain it.

Endless effort, no gain.

And then it's over. I leave, put on my shoes, and walk in the sun to the rented car.

The homeless men have not budged from the picnic table. They go through their motions and I go through mine, I think. If you go through the motions enough (for example, every Sunday), does something happen? It's a question that lingers in my mind for two days, at the end of which I realize that I have a preconceived notion of what this "something" is. I have an unconscious expectation. A mental block that prevents me from understanding. In other words, a devil.

I feel compelled to call my sister Mary to discuss this, but when she asks, "Well, what do you think there is to get?" I explode into irrational tears. My throat cramps, and I mumble, "I cannot talk about this." But in my heart I know the answer.

I want to know, one-hundred percent, that what Shirley went through was worth it. I want one-hundred percent assurance that I will understand death, find God, and live happily ever after. I want to revise the Sensei's message: a little effort, endless gain.

In other words, I have to face this devil.

Saturday

I wake up moaning, "I don't know who it is! I don't know who it is!" This has happened to me periodically for over three years. In my sleep, I am often burdened with a sense of deep responsibility. I know I am supposed to take care of someone, and I know I am not doing the job. Many nights, I have sat bolt upright in the dark, snapped out of sleep by panic, and said, "Who? Who?" Then, last July, after I went east to take care of Shirley, I had the dream (I call it a dream, even if it is mostly a feeling), but this time I was in a dark corridor and at the end of it was a door. "I know I'm supposed to be taking care of someone, but I don't know who it is," I whispered as I walked toward this dream door in a trance, hugging the wall and moving very slowly. When I got there, the door was ajar, maybe two inches. I pushed it and it creaked open.

And there was Shirley. She looked like she did at the end—a skeleton—though at the time of the dream, I had no idea of what was to come for her. I woke up screaming, terrified, sobbing. "It was Shirley,"

I mumbled to Robert, who had woken up, too—of course, with all the screaming—and was rubbing my lower back. "All this time, it was Shirley." I did not have to tell him what I was talking about. He has seen me jolt awake in a panic many nights. Heard me say "I don't know who it is" in the darkness.

Over the months and years that I have had this dream, I have made a mental list of those whom I thought, perhaps, I had to save. At first, they were all aspects of myself: the writer inside me who could not find time to write; the artist whose sculptures, built from fallen trees along the dog-walking path by the Rio Grande, needed attention; the hippie who was living the straight life. Other times, I thought maybe I had to save Robert, a student, some friend, or sick people in third world countries. I never thought of Shirley, even during the last year when she started to have such intense back pains that she had to get up in the night to soak in a hot tub. For this severe pain, her doctor had recommended over-the-counter Tylenol. "How bad is the pain?" I asked Shirley when I went to visit her in May. "On a scale of one to ten, with childbirth at ten, how bad is it?" "A ten," she said, looking down so I would not see her tears.

In that moment, I wanted to kill her doctor.

So when that dream-door finally opened and I saw Shirley, I felt wretched and ashamed, even though in reality I was there, taking care of her. The dreams had started three years before. Maybe I could have done something if I had known it was Shirley I was supposed to take care of. But now she's gone, and I have had this dream again.

"Now who?" I say into the chilly air in my *casita*. I get up and walk around. The concrete floor is cold, and the refrigerator rattles loudly. "Now who?" I say louder, angrily.

On my kitchen table is an essay by Julia Kristeva called "Woman Time" which I have just read. In it, she calls for a revision in our way of thinking about time. Linear time, with its accoutrements of progress, direction, product, and goal orientation, is beginning to fray around the edges as a concept, she says. She suggests that we switch over immediately to "woman time" which is based not in production but in reproduction, and stresses cyclical movement, repetition, and notions of eternity. In woman time, things don't end. They repeat. They come around again. They are never finished. There is no climax, no closure, no end.

Endless effort, no gain.

Now who?

At the end of my job with Shirley, after she died but before the funeral, I went over to her house, where all her kids and all their kids had gathered. It was crowded, as it always was at Shirley's before they grew up and scattered. The Christmas tree, which Kim had put up in a supreme act of courage during the two weeks she spent there just before Shirley took the Final Dive, was twinkling with colored lights and handmade ornaments, each one with a family story. There was food, given by Shirley's friends, and laughter.

I was sitting on the floor in the living room when I heard the kids whisper, "Should we do it now?" And then, everyone started to sing—to me:

> Happy trails to you, until we meet again.
> Happy trails to you, keep smiling until then.
> Happy trails to you, till we meet again

—the theme song to the old Roy Rogers Show, which I loved as a kid, and which I sang to them and they sang back to me every time I came or went from Shirley's house during the hippie years, and after. At every little ending.

They formed a line, starting with Billy's son, Alan, and filed past me. Alan placed a cooler in my lap and opened it. Then Andrew, Billy's older son, filed by and put a one-pound bag of peanut M&Ms in it. One by one, they marched by, still singing "Happy Trails." And at this little end, I had:

> a cooler
> two one-pound bags of peanut M&Ms
> one one-pound bag of plain M&Ms
> a six-pack of caffeine free Diet Pepsi
> a road atlas
> a bag of food for my dog, Maggie
> the latest *Mad* magazine
> gas cards to pay for my whole trip back to New Mexico.

And, of course, Shirley's car to make the trip in.

I laughed until my sides hurt. Looking past them all, out the window at the deep snow, I yelled. "I'm getting out! I'm finally getting out!" We all laughed more. Harder.

I had told my nephew Jimmy the week before that I felt like a gunslinger in the Old West. I had come to town to clean it up and now the job was almost done. When it was, I would shove my guns back in my holster, climb on my horse, and move on. "Sh-a-a-a-ne!" he called from his position on the couch, prone, doing a logic problem.

But as I looked around in that moment, I thought that, right then, despite my words, I wanted to stay with them, this close, forever.

Never go away.

Not have it end.

Woman time.

The First Church of Religious Science
Albuquerque, NM

T he service at the First Church of Religious Science begins at eleven. I drive across town in the car I bought yesterday after I miraculously managed to get a car loan, which I really didn't expect, what with my graduate student status and my spotty history of car ownership. I feel very smart in my almost-new Mazda, but before I am even two miles from home, the "Check Engine" light comes on. At a stop sign, I yank the Owner's Manual out of the glove compartment and find the "Check Engine" section in the index. I do this in a red rage that makes me ignore that dashboard light and drive on—speed, even—toward church. So what if the manual advises an immediate trip to the mechanic? So what if you can't count on a new car to act right for twenty-four hours? So what if you can't count on anything at all? So what?

I pull into the lot at the Church of Religious Science, annoyed that it actually is a church, complete with double doors and a steeple. Because of the word "science," I expected a wood-paneled meeting room, or perhaps a library with Ayn Rand novels open in the carrels. Instead, I get a Norman Rockwell painting. A smiling old-timer using a walker negotiates the ramp toward the open door, and kids on skateboards zoom around the parking lot and up and down the cement sides of the irrigation ditch.

Impatiently, I go inside. Same old set-up: the platform with a grand piano, a stand-up bass, a drum set, and a podium in the center. There is a statue of an eagle with its wings outspread and a circular painting of the curl of a wave or perhaps Planet Earth from outer space. I have to climb over several people to get to a center seat, and soon musicians arrive and begin to play jazz. Within minutes, the church transforms into a night club. Musicians wail and the congregation conversates, as the prisoners I know would put it. In my twenties, I spent a few years waiting tables in great jazz clubs like Paul's Mall in Boston and Sweet Basil in New York, and I am fluent in how they feel and sound. This one is as authentic as it can possibly be, minus smoke and booze. My shoulders drop a few inches and begin to move with the music. I look around. Instead of live-action photos of jazz legends on the walls, there are banners with uplifting messages: I am aware, I am connected, I am prosperous, I am love, I am joy, I am light. Am I light? I certainly feel lighter than I did a few minutes ago.

The music ends and in strolls the Reverend H. Patrick Pollard, definitely the sexiest preacher I've ever seen. Tall, handsome, and elegant, he wears a grey suit right out of *GQ*, complete with a white shirt and a scarlet handkerchief. He is of indeterminate race—something which I find intensely fascinating. So far, I have met only three such mystery-blend people in my life: one male judge in L.A. when I was on jury duty, one female Aikido instructor, from whom I took two private lessons in Venice, CA, and one female inmate at Riker's Island, who was my student (and my teacher). I like such racial ambiguity. I wish I had some of it myself.

Reverend Patrick leads us in today's affirmation, which is printed in the bulletin:

> Our loving church is a thriving community that demonstrates the nature of the One Source. Today I am conscious of the Divine Embrace; as each moment unfolds I sense more deeply the warmth and assurance of unconditional

love. I allow this love to be fully expressed in all that I do. I am love. And so it is.

Then he smiles and says in a slight accent, maybe British, "Just sit back and open yourself to the spirit." I remember making that promise to myself, those exact words, as I started off on my first Sunday. So I do it: I sit back and open myself to the spirit.

Obviously for my benefit, Reverend Patrick's "Message from the Heart" is entitled "Who's Driving Your Car?" I don't particularly want to be reminded of cars because they always break down on me. Before Shirley gave me her Escort, I borrowed it one day when my Colt was in the shop, and it crapped out within five minutes and had to be towed away. (At forty-nine years old, I had to hitchhike to my teaching job that day.) And last week, when I was in New York for spring break, the Colt was out of commission again, and while I was driving Shirley's Escort, I had a blowout. Jungians (like I used to be) believe that cars in dreams symbolize the "personal vehicle" of the dreamer. If that crosses over into real life, then I'm playing it too fast and too loose with my personal vehicles. I drive them on bald tires, forget to change the oil, wait until the last possible moment to get gas. I know I'd best listen up as Reverend Patrick begins.

We all have potential, he says, if we learn to direct the Universal Mind. Like a car without a driver, our potential, the Mind, waits to be of service to us. All we have to do is get into the driver's seat and turn it on. If we steer with consciousness, we can arrive at any destination we choose, but to drive well, we have to know exactly who we are. If things do not go right, we must ask ourselves this question: To what have I given unconscious agreement to act for me in my life?

Reverend Patrick has created an acronym for CAR: cognition (having the information, or knowing where we want to go), acquiescence (accepting that we must work in a certain way to get there), and release (letting go. Giving it to God). Life is a journey, he reminds us, and then he concludes with, "I hope this week you find a way to let your mind take you where you want to go."

We join together in a hymn unlike any other I have ever sung in any church:

LIFE IS A BLAST!
(Lyrics by Evelyn Hammond; music by Holly Addy)

Life is a blast! Life is a ball!
But life without love is no life at all.
So, look at the birds, and look at the bees
and celebrate life where ever you please.

Make the first move, and step out in love.
Trust and believe then go with the flow
and celebrate life, and celebrate love.
Where ever you are.

Because,
Life is a blast! Life is a ball!
and life without love is no life at all!
Look at the birds, and look at the bees
And celebrate life where ever you please.

I belt this out as loud as I possibly can because I deeply want to believe that life is a blast and life is a ball. Afterward, Reverend Patrick croons us a prayer, and no joke, he sounds just like Johnny Hartman. I close my eyes and just listen.

At the end of the service, during the "Peace Song," Reverend Patrick moves to the rear of the church. He calls out phrases, which we repeat. I remember only the last two:

I accept life for what it is. (We repeat.)

And what it isn't. (We repeat.)

Amen.

I sit in my new Mazda in the parking lot. There is water in the concrete ditch now and everyone whose car, like mine, is parked along the edge stands and watches it flow for a few moments. Water flowing through the desert. It's a beautiful thing.

Just before I turn on the ignition, I pray for a small miracle. I want my CAR to go. I turn the key. It starts up.

"Check Engine," it says.

I laugh all the way home.

Thursday

Recently, I had lunch with Sharon Oard Warner, who asked me why my sister was a hermit. I think I said, "Because that was the way she was. That was Shirley." Once, I wrote somewhere that after her kids grew up, she drew a magic circle around her house and never left it, except for necessities. When Neal, the baby of the family, went away to college, I asked Shirley this question: "So now that it's basically a wrap, what do you think of motherhood?" She hesitated as if she were at an inner crossroads, unsure which way to take. Then she said, "It's not my bag."

"It's not your bag?" I repeated. This was probably in 1988, long after the sixties when that expression fell from my own lips at least ten times a week. "How long have you known this?"

"I just figured it out," she said, and then we both drank instant coffee in silence for a long time. A minute is a long time when both people in the room are floored.

"Well, you did a great job," I finally mumbled, noticing how quiet the house was with the kids all gone. Billy, Julie, John, Kim, and Neal, off to college or graduate school or work, and Jimmy off to the Navy, underwater somewhere in a nuclear submarine.

"I did the best I could," Shirley said. I think she said that, though maybe she said nothing and I am remembering an alternate version, one that I am supplying to fill in the silence in her kitchen all those years ago.

What does this have to do with hermithood?

Just this: a hermit with six kids does not appear to be a hermit, but take away the children and the truth emerges, like a volcanic island that for geological reasons suddenly asserts itself above the surface of the sea. Now I think about the way Shirley removed herself from the world, how she found her way to her isolated farmhouse in 1970, how she chose the most remote house on the real estate market at the time. The farmer who had lived there had had enough of it and intended to move into town for his old age.

"Pa is gonna be dead soon," his middle-aged daughter said, right in front of her father. For years when I would call Shirley, I would ask, "Well, is Pa dead yet?" and she would always answer no. And then once she said yes. Pa's daughter, Bea, came to visit Shirley several times when she was sick. She brought little boxes of fruit juice with attached straws and gave them to Shirley as gifts. When she emerged from Shirley's room the first time, I worried that she might say, "Shirley's gonna be dead soon," but she didn't.

Pa sold the farm to Shirley on a land contract: $110 a month for ten years. No money down, as I recall. And Shirley's husband, the hotshot pilot, went off to a year in Vietnam. There was trouble in the marriage. Booze and other women. When he came back, he promised to reform but within days of making this promise, when he was away from home for a few days on air force business, Shirley got a phone call from a woman in a motel room. "Just so you know the truth," this woman whispered. And then she called out Shirley's husband's name.

He responded from the shower.

That day, Shirley called our sister Mary, who also lived in the North Country that year because her husband was in Vietnam, too. They went to a little park by a river, where all ten of their children could play. Mary and Shirley sat on a picnic table.

Shirley sobbed and sobbed.

Life is a blast. Life is a ball.

And then Shirley asked for a divorce.

Last summer, she said that up until that point, she was willing to give her marriage one more shot provided her husband was willing to change. But he wasn't. And he lied.

Repeat after me: Life is a blast. Life is a ball.

In a letter, my sister Mary told me that when Shirley first found out about her husband's infidelity, when she was a young wife with two infants just arrived in Okinawa, she talked to a priest on base who told her that one day, a door would open for her, and when it did, she should take her children and leave the marriage. It didn't open for more than a decade, but when it did, Shirley rushed through.

She stayed in her old, isolated farmhouse, a beautiful woman with a radiant smile and a laugh that warmed you, even in winter. She stayed alone with six children, in the middle of nowhere, and her life was very hard. Her youngest, Neal, was sickly. The house was too small, and she had to do all the repairs herself. Almost every morning in the winter, she put on her husband's flight suit and disappeared into the cellar crawlspace to unfreeze the water pipes with a hair drier. Money was scarce.

When it ran out, she got a minimum wage job in the county nursing home, and worked there for twenty-two years.

But Shirley endured. She began to thrive, in a way. She bought old furniture in junk shops and restored it. Slowly, she transformed her house into an antique museum. "Isn't this beautiful?" she would say when she showed me something she had just redone. Just like Laurie's dream.

Alone, she raised her six children.

Began to plant flowers.

Retired from the nursing home.

Got cancer of the pancreas.

Died on Christmas night.

My sister.

She accepted life for what it is. And what it isn't.

The Salvation Army
Albuquerque, NM

This week I pick the Salvation Army, the source of one of my top ten all-time best visuals: twenty years ago, I was on the Number 6 train in New York when the door opened at the Bowery and no fewer than twenty-five bums got on, all in one-piece Santa Claus jumpsuits, complete with elastic stirrups. Each one held a brass bell. It was so much like being in a kooky dream that I didn't even laugh. And once, in Los Angeles, my friend Starr told me that she had just received a precious gift from her grandmother, who, she said, was "in the army." Being raised at West Point, I knew too well the meaning of the word "army," and imagined her gift was, perhaps, a purple heart in a box lined with blue velvet or a visored cap with full-bird brass across the front, but her grandmother, also named Starr, was actually a Salvation Army officer, and the gift was her personal Bible.

It takes dedication to get to the Salvation Army Center for Worship and Service because Bryn Mawr, like many streets in Albuquerque, comes to frequent dead ends and then starts up again, farther north. I arrive at three such endings before I finally find the place, arriving there just five minutes early. Two little girls, dressed up like I used to have to for church—white dress with crinoline, white socks, patent leather Mary Janes—hand out programs. They both look so anxious to succeed at their job that I take the identical program from each.

This is a plain church with a cross in front (no hanging Jesus); a couple organs, one of which is being played by a Salvation Army lady in a starched white shirt with epaulets; a podium, some chairs facing the congregation, and a table covered with books. A few men wear ratty full-dress uniforms. The congregation is primarily non-white. It is packed, and I move forward to the fifth row before I find a pew to share with a young Hispanic couple observing the *cholo* fashion guidelines— he, shaved head and baggy pants; she, permed hair and a tattoo. He sits with his leg slung over hers and they clutch each other's hands tightly.

The Holiness Meeting begins with the song: "This Is the Day the Lord Has Made." The singing here is thin, very thin, the star vocalist being a woman with a wobbly voice who sits directly behind me. She sounds, as my mother would say, like a dying calf in a thunderstorm. Not that I do any better. When it finally fizzles out totally, Captain George Beauchamp, the ranking officer, I presume, says that we have some "Completions" to witness.

Three men are called to the front of the church: a Hispanic with grey hair; a young Hispanic, maybe thirty, wearing a crisp white shirt; and an old, skinny white guy. They have all reached six months of sobriety and therefore completed the Salvation Army program. One by one, they address us from the podium to give thanks, accept prayers, and ask for help. The older Hispanic man is especially grateful, he says, to have the false teeth the Salvation Army has provided. "Now I can smile at the world," he adds, proving it. He pauses thoughtfully and then continues. "Last week, I got a job at Wal-Mart. I never worked so hard in my life. Pray for me that I can hold up." The young Hispanic man announces that he is ready to move into a halfway house with a "sober environ-ment." The white man thanks "all the guys who befriended me when I didn't even know who I was or where I was."

This Completion Ceremony is truly heart-wrenching. I'm a sucker for redemption stories, and the farther down the protagonist, the higher the resurrection. A job at Wal-Mart is a peak and I know it. But these men look so happy, healthy, and proud, it's difficult to imagine them as potential Santas. Realizing this, several minutes into the Completions, I take a closer look at the congregation, which is mostly male. Now that I focus, I see spiderweb tattoos on elbows, scorpions at the base of the neck, and even two "Born to Lose" announcements on biceps. One guy has a black eye. There are more serious scars here than I've seen anywhere but prison.

(One time, I asked another teacher in a medium security joint if she knew a particular inmate. "What does he look like?" she asked. "He's the tall black guy with the big scar from a slit throat," I said. "Which one?" she responded.)

Then I notice the odd pairs in the congregation: an old white lady with a young black man; a blow-dried, middle-aged white guy with a *cholo* in his twenties. I realize these are counselors or support people. Suddenly, it hits me that this normal-looking group is actually a platoon of warriors, fighting those devils I keep hearing about, shape-shifted into alcohol this time, and I feel ashamed of myself for coming here almost as a joke.

It is no joke what these men are saying.

No joke what the Salvation Army is doing to help them.

There is a Bible reading, another prayer, and several songs. We don't get any better at singing them either, and Captain Beauchamp is so disgusted with us that he makes us repeat one whole hymn, and do it louder, better, and with more feeling. Next, we hear a little speech on time. Time has been measured in three ways in history, he says: world time, which is organized according to the movement of the planets; atomic time, started in 1972, based on the vibration of atoms, which is news to me; and perfect time, which is centered in our relationship to God. God must be kept in every hour, every minute, every second, he says, and then concludes with this sentence: "If we are going to live honestly and lovingly, in perfect time, we have to do it now."

I experience a little thud in my chest. There is so much to do in the now, I think. No wonder people start drinking.

Next is another hymn "with testimonials," which means that we sing a verse, after which anyone who wants to stands up and testifies. "I thank God for letting me find the Salvation Army," one man says. "I thank God for letting me have clean clothes." "I thank God for helping me endure this program." (We all laugh at that one.) The men give thanks for jobs, prayers, friendship, their families. They give thanks for the sunrise, sunset, and the flowers that have burst forth all over Albuquerque. They give thanks for having food, having teeth with which to eat it, being alive. One handsome man, sitting in the row in front of me and looking very dapper all in black, says, "Acceptance. Strength. Freedom." The Salvation Army members, the helpers to these men, thank God for leading them to service in the Army, for the opportunity to meet these wonderful and worthy men, for the chance to go into prisons and provide comfort and guidance. In between, we sing—if it can be called that—another verse.

As if this isn't enough to break my heart, a lone man comes forward to sing us a country-western song—something that centers on lifting his hand to the Lord. Before he begins, he says that his arm was torn almost right off him a while back, and it was the Salvation Army and the Lord that gave him the strength to recover. He puts on a tape for musical accompaniment, and each time he raises that right arm, during the chorus when his motion mimics the words, I am flooded. He finishes and returns to the seat behind me. "I was so nervous," he whispers to the woman with the wobbly voice.

Today's "message," delivered by Captain Beauchamp, is that, while we might desert Jesus, he will never desert us. No matter what we've done, he says, Jesus is always there for us if we just turn toward him. This relationship to God is necessarily emotional, he says. "If we don't have an emotional relationship with God, there's something wrong in our lives." Then he adds, very quietly, "If you don't have an emotional relationship with God, you belong here right now," and he points to a bench across the front of the church.

A young white guy slowly moves toward this bench. I expect him to sit, but he kneels on the floor in front of it, folds his hands on it, and collapses forward over it. Three others follow, including the "Acceptance. Strength. Freedom" guy who seemed so powerful when he testified. I remember the bowing I saw and did in the zen center two weeks ago. There, the bowing was symbolic, a ritualized demonstration of the willingness of the ego to be humble for a minute. But here it isn't like that. Here, it's about begging for mercy. It's about defeat and helplessness. It's about no ego at all.

I cry until the top of my dress is damp. A Salvation Army woman leads us in a special prayer for these men, and I say (to God?), if I have any healing energy left after Shirley to pass on, please let me give it to these battered souls.

Shirley had no patience for drunks. The first time her young husband came home plastered and collapsed into a heap on the bathroom floor, she left him there all night. In May, when I went back for a visit, back to hustle the doctors who did not seem to take her case seriously, a young resident routinely asked her how much alcohol she consumed. "I've never had a drink in my life," she answered. He seemed shocked, even though he came from a culture (Arab) that frowns on drinking. "Ask me if I've ever had any fun," she added, "and the answer is no." This was the day Shirley and I ordered the blood test for cancer markers in the pancreatic enzymes. The resident was reluctant to do it, but succumbed to our pressure. Shirley wore a pink and white seersucker dress from K-Mart. When this young doctor asked her her profession, she said, "I was a nurse's aide. And," she seemed to hesitate for a few beats. "...and I raised a family," she said.

"Six kids," I chimed in. Not to mention me.

We say the Benediction, which is printed in the program:

> Give to Jesus Glory
> Give to Jesus Glory
> Proclaim redemption's wondrous plan
> And give to Jesus glory.

We leave. Salvation Army men and women wait in the doorway to shake each hand, everybody's hand, and thank us all, thank me, for coming.

I sit in my new car, which has been repaired free of charge by the dealer, and watch the men from the church cross the parking lot to load into Salvation Army vans and buses. How many of them will make it to the Completion Ceremony, I wonder. I hope they do. Every single one.

Myself, I stopped drinking five years ago.

Tuesday

I still feel shaky from my Salvation Army Sunday, as if I had the DTs, on Tuesday, when I meet my friend Whitney at noon at Duran's

Pharmacy. I like the lunch counter there, which is run by women with western accents and specializes in meals served with or on huge flour tortillas. Our food comes quickly: tortilla and chili pepper soup for her, and, for me, a torpedo, which consists of potatoes, red chili, and cheese wrapped up in a tortilla and smothered in hot sauce. We eat heartily among men in cowboy hats who take their coffee black.

Days after I got back to New Mexico in January, I told Whitney, before anyone else, that I felt strangely compelled to go to church. She remembers that and asks me if I've gone. I explain how my Shirley memories and my *Sundays* have merged. How I sometimes feel that I am taking Shirley to church every Sunday, trying to find a place for her in which there is no hell to torture herself with. No purgatory to burn in just before you die.

Last week, while reading *A Rhetoric of Motives* by Kenneth Burke, I came upon a passage in which he quotes Pico Della Mirandola's Latin text, "On the Imagination":

> Children are mostly motivated by the brutish kind of the imagination. Hence, and because of their weak intellects, one best guides them in the way of virtue by bringing them to imagine in detail the tortures of hell...

Reading that, I pictured Shirley, a Catholic school girl, imagining in detail the tortures of hell. And having it all come rushing back to her in Stage Two of the Final Dive, just before she died. But I do not reveal all this to Whitney because I do not want to rant like a fanatic about hell over lunch, especially given the heat of this year's chili crop.

I change the subject instead. "Remember that Navajo grandfather who came to see me at UNM?" I ask.

Whitney leans back and nods.

To Whitney, it must seem like a random conversational tangent, but inside I am working hard to neutralize the images of hell that periodically assert themselves in my mind ever since Shirley worried about going there during the Final Dive. Once, the day of the Navajo grandfather, I personally experienced heaven, right here on earth, and I use this memory to keep the fires of hell at bay.

"He completely changed me."

"How?" Whitney asks.

"He told me the story of his life," I answer.

I am remembering Leroy Begay, who showed up in the o..... shared with Whitney fifteen months ago to ask me a few school-related questions about ESL classes. In my mind, he settles into the orange bucket chair, his Lobos cap low on his forehead and his feet barely touching the ground, and somehow he begins to tell me his story. Maybe I have blatantly asked him, surprised as I am that a sixty-two year old Native man would be a college student, living in the dorms like a teenager. I may have said, "How did you get here?", though I don't recall.

"How?" Whitney asks, and when I look at her blankly, she adds, "How did his story change your life?"

"It was a story of falling, falling for years, of hitting rock bottom, and then rising up." I think I am mumbling. I am so lost in a memory.

As Leroy talks, my insides, behind my ribcage, start to shudder. The internal shaking becomes so violent that I think for sure he can see it, but he gives no indication if he does. I feel somehow that he is telling not only his story but mine. The details don't matter. As he describes waking up, his own resurrection, I feel filled with hope, with certainty even, that I can wake up, too. That some part of my life that's shrouded in darkness can come into the light, and nothing will ever be the same again. I am not thinking about this. I am experiencing it.

His words lift me out of my office, my self, and my life and transport me to a more amazing world. Just before I slip into it completely, I remember how, back in L.A. in the temple of tarot, we were often encouraged to trust in an esoteric principle: When the student is ready, the teacher will arrive. It is unquestionable to me, this moment in my office, that my teacher has arrived, especially given the severe shaking inside my torso.

I learn that Leroy is an artist exactly Shirley's age. He invites me to his dorm room to see a painting in which he recounts his life. I sit on his narrow cot, amazed, and study every inch of the canvas. At the center is a large circle of gold with a braid around it. The bottom arc of the circle, perhaps ten or fifteen percent of the circumference, is left unbraided. "This is the life I've lived so far," he says, pointing to the braid. "This is what I have left."

I feel a sudden panic. "It doesn't look like very much," I say. Shirley flashes into my mind in this instant. I don't know it that day in his dorm room, but—maybe even as I sit there—Shirley is facing up to the truth that she is very sick. She has serious pain in her back and other symptoms. She first admits them—to her daughter Julie, I think—a few days later, at Thanksgiving.

In Leroy's room, I start to sob uncontrollably. I don't want him, whom I have only known for a few hours, to die, and I don't want to think of Shirley's braid as all but finished. He stands calmly near the doorway to his room, as if it is totally routine to witness a woman possessed with an unexpected fear of death melt down before his painting.

I leave. I skip my afternoon classes and go down to the Rio Grande to work on my sculptures. Every leaf in the cottonwoods shimmers and the black crows that fill their branches look surrealistically huge. When one perches directly overhead, I look up and say, "Leroy?" (He is in the bird clan.) I sit for hours, higher by far than I have ever been, on the bank of the river. Thanks to Leroy Begay, to the power of his story, I feel it when my heart sheds its skin. I even turn around once to look behind me, expecting to see a heart-shaped membrane in my wake.

I still do not know for sure what happened to me. I felt bursting with light, with love, with joy. I felt my cells could not even begin to contain it. Life, my life, that moment—it was supremely perfect in every way. I remained in that altered state for several days. My friend Julie Reichert later commented that I acted like a Born Again Christian—a monumental insult, I thought at the time—but I simply couldn't help it. I was flooded with confidence, with complete certainty, that each individual life, the ups and downs included, is magnificent.

I have thought long and hard on that day, studied it from outside the experience but inside the memories, and it remains a mystery. But the mystery isn't *why* it happened: I have figured out that part. Leroy showed me that a good story, a well told, true story of despair and resurrection, has the power to heal. Every honest storyteller knows this, and every listener counts on it. When the chemistry is right, when the listener is so absorbed in the story that she completely forgets who she is, a little opening is created, and she can squeeze through into a parallel universe. That parallel universe is right here, but usually inaccessible. Somehow, Leroy's simple storytelling and my deep listening combined to get me there.

What I would like to understand but can't is *what* happened.
my senses intensify so dramatically, and my heart fill to burst
love? How did time disappear? How did my happiness become
plete that even the memory of it soothes me? I have concluded that
what I experienced was a moment of grace—my own personal
moment, full of grace—and it transformed me. I didn't have to believe
anything. I knew that I'd been set free in some basic, crucial way.

In my spiritual life, that day was, hands down, the peak.

I do not tell Whitney that it has not been repeated in church, and I
do not tell her how Shirley's return to Catholicism brought with it fear
and the fires of hell—not love, light, and beauty.

Instead, I confide that Sharon Oard Warner asked me why Shirley
was a hermit, and strangely, ever since, I have been a little afraid. If I
answer that question, I say, the story may take its own Final Dive, and
I will have to let it.

Whitney leans forward and whispers, "Well, why *was* she a
hermit?"

I stir a whirlpool into my coffee and then mumble, "I think she was
scared."

I am scared now.

"Every person wants someone to listen to her story," Whitney says
with the confidence of the writer she is. "You have to tell her story for
her." A second later she adds, very softly, "Then maybe she won't have
to be scared anymore."

I have shredded my paper napkin but I use it anyway to wipe my
eyes. "Emotional tidal wave passing," I whisper.

Shirley's story. Leroy's story. Mine. They all whirl through me until I
begin to wonder if they are some new form of religious text. A Bible just
for me.

Saturday

I had a dream.

I was at a beach and somebody—maybe Robert—was explaining to
me that energy is always rolling under the surface of existence. That is
what, this person says, the waves of the sea tumble over. This energy has

its own logic with its own schedule to keep. This other person—or being—in the dream and I are studying the water and watching the waves break. I can feel cold water on my feet. I get the idea that this mystery energy is released with each wave that breaks, and in the dream, I feel that I am starting to understand something important: "The waves break where they will," I say, and I know this has to do with Shirley dying. With every person dying. I feel rather amazed and I turn to this person, but for some reason I get distracted and look down at my left hand. On it, I wear an engagement ring. I have a very precise memory of the ring. It is a slab of silver, like the moon, very wide on my finger, and thick. The edges are not beveled. Rising from it are curved prongs like tiny silver fingers, offering up a huge diamond. I notice that the diamond is loose and when I touch it with my right hand, it breaks off.

In the dream, I say, "The engagement...it's over."

And I'm thinking, All I have now is the diamond.

I wake up feeling extraordinarily good. Very happy.

Outside in our yard, I recount the dream to Julie Reichert. It takes a long time, and we both end up sitting on the ground. I tell her, too, for the first time, about how back in November I told Shirley that I was going to leave in January, about how I can't forgive myself for it, but somehow this dream is helping. She listens like Shirley did. She reminds me of Shirley. Has, ever since I met her.

Then she says, "It's one thing to ask for forgiveness. But it's another to feel forgiven." A pause. "Do you feel forgiven?"

I consider this for a minute. "I don't think in those terms. I think in terms of, Does it make sense? And now, after the dream, it makes sense. Waves are on their own schedule, and they break where they break," I say. "It applies to me, too."

The engagement is broken.

But I have the diamond.

If I have hurt you, Shirley, I ask you to forgive me.

I invite Julie inside and show her the pictures my niece and I took of Shirley in Stage Three of the Final Dive. I keep these pictures seriously hidden. I haven't had the courage to look at them in months, but now we spread them out on the dresser top. They are brutal. They are stunning. We are both stunned by the waves that broke over Shirley.

The Corn Dance
Pueblo de Cochiti, NM

NO PHOTO
PERMITTED

My buddy Judith Van Gieson, a mystery writer who holes up in her North Valley home and murders imaginary people for fun and profit, has invited me to attend the Corn Dance at the Pueblo de Cochiti. It seems odd to do a Sunday with another person, and I mull it over at length before I decide to go. Today is Easter—a good day to attend a Corn Dance. A good day to spend with a good friend. A good day to be outside, among people to whom all of nature is one big church. Besides, I feel somewhat resurrected myself after my diamond dream, and therefore more social. We head north. Judith has an acquaintance, a Native elder named Mary, who has extended this invitation to us. It is an honor to be invited.

When we arrive in Pueblo de Cochiti, all around the square, Native people sit under portals and on porches and some have set up folding chairs on the flat roofs of the adobe houses. Along one side of the *centro* are wide steps, like a terrace, and several visitors have settled there. Because we are with Mary, though, we are allowed to sit on a plank bench, our backs resting against the mud wall of an adobe house. Busy dogs without collars trot back and forth in front of us. Sometimes they roll or tumble in the red dirt.

No pictures are permitted here, and I am hesitant to describe the Corn Dance in English words. The people of Cochiti do not trust words. They speak not-much and have never written down their language. When another visitor, a man from Hawaii who looks Japanese, quizzes Mary on the symbolic significance of the costumes and movements, she answers every question with, "I don't know. It's a Corn Dance." Like many other Native women, Mary sits wrapped in a colorful shawl. Hers is magenta with fringe; others are batik or bold floral prints. They use these shawls to protect themselves from the sun and to cover their heads and faces when the wind whips up the sand. The younger women do not wear them, I notice. I find myself wistfully hoping that they will grow into them later, but I have my doubts. Like Shirley's hairdo, shawls are becoming a thing of the past.

I remember how, when Shirley's hair began to seriously fall out and she no longer had the strength to lift her comb to tease it, I brushed it, parted it in the middle, and braided it into two spindly plaits, Indian style. I thought she looked striking and handed her a mirror. "Now there's a face that would scare you," she said, and then, little by little over many hours, she painstakingly rebuilt her Gibson Girl hairdo. We sprayed it until it was as hard as varnish. Sometimes I would tap it and say "Knock, knock," as a joke. I look at Elder Mary. Her long grey hair, neither teased nor sprayed, is the color Shirley's was. It shimmers like a silver halo when the bright sun hits it at the right angle.

Soon, there is the sound of the drum, and a group of men enters the square in a tight unit, chanting the private stories that keep their culture alive. They hop from foot to foot, are never still. Some carry babies in their arms. Then women and girls, young men and boys, dance into the square. The females wear one-shouldered black dresses, moccasins, and wooden *tablita* headdresses. They carry pine boughs in each hand. The young males (some with shaved heads or fade haircuts) wear white kilts, shells bandolier-style across their bare chests, and bells on their waists, wrists, and ankles. Pine boughs are tucked into their armbands, and animal skins, like tails, sway behind them. From the bench, we hear chanting, rattling shells, and bells; we see feet dancing in the sand. The same dance, in the same sand, for a thousand years. Sometimes wind whips up, and the watching women cover their faces with their flowered shawls.

Hour after hour, they dance in the blazing desert sun. I wish I could understand the words to the songs, relive the stories along with the dancers. The Native American writer Leslie Marmon Silko, who comes from a Pueblo not far from here, says that Indian stories are constructed like a spider's web, "with many little threads radiating from the center, crisscrossing each other. As with the web, the structure emerges as it is made and you must simply listen and trust, as the Pueblo people do, that the meaning will be made."

Remembering this, I relax into a sense of peace about my Sunday quest. There is no hurry, not really. Maybe it will all become clear, if I just listen and trust.

I sit back and observe the dance, the prayer to the Great Spirit that the corn will grow. It is mesmerizing, meditative. After a long, long time in suspended animation, I stand up. I know I'm not allowed in the *centro* and I wouldn't even think of placing one toe into the hot sand there, but I move around the corner of the adobe. Just for a second, I imagine myself in a black dress and *tablita*. Hidden, certain that no one in this world can see me, I dance. Just two steps.

But this Sunday, I dance.

Friday

Yesterday I asked two close friends, one after the other, if they believed in God. It was strange to ask that question, given that I have known these women for so long. I have known them for decades, intimately. I know their values, their relationship history, what makes them tick. I know their attitudes toward the government, UFOs, and education. I know what books they read, what movies they like, and which foods are their favorites.

But I never knew that neither one believes in God.

I have decided not to ask anyone else for a while.

Christ in the Desert Benedictine Monastery
Abiquiu, NM

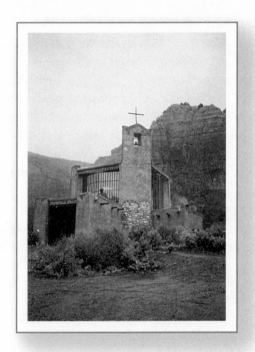

I have come to Christ in the Desert, a Benedictine monastery, for a silent weekend retreat. This week, I will attend Sunday mass in the quietest place on earth. The monastery is thirteen miles down a dirt road filled with stones, ruts, and dangerous curves. For three miles, the road is only wide enough for one car, and if you meet someone coming, which you won't, you have to back up into tiny turn-outs. I have been here three times before, drawn back by the humbling beauty and the pervasive silence. The information posted on the website warns that some visitors, used to living in a noise culture, experience fear of this quiet.

I arrive just in time for vespers, whatever vespers are, and hurry along the clay road to the church where the monks gather for hours, many times per day. Inside, they sing "This Is the Day the Lord Has Made," which I last heard at the Salvation Army service. Seventeen monks, eight nuns, and ten guests have gathered in this simple church with high red cliffs visible out every window. I study the faces of those who have chosen the silent path. Even though they spend their entire lives contemplating life, God, and whatever monks and nuns contemplate, they look relatively normal. After vespers, we go to the dining room for dinner. No one speaks, though one monk reads junk mail at the table.

I walk back to my room slowly, breathing in the peace, the quiet, the spectacular, breathtaking beauty, and fall asleep by eight. Even so, I sleep straight through the four a.m. bell. When the six o'clock bell rings, though, I bolt out of bed, slip into jeans, sneakers, and a shirt, and run out the door within a minute. Halfway to the church, it hits me that I haven't lit my Shirley candle, which I have brought with me and placed on the simple wooden table by the bed. It bothers me to be jolted out of my morning routine, but I continue on. The monks and nuns, looking rested, sing Gregorian chants with gusto. Then we have breakfast: a slice of bread and coffee for me, though there is also oatmeal and hard-boiled eggs. I return to my room, but at nine, I'm back in church again, and afterward I volunteer for "manual labor," which the monks recommend as part of the Christ in the Desert experience.

I get two jobs. The first is to clean the wax out of the votive candle holders, scrub them clean, and place fresh candles in them. I evoke the spirit of Shirley to do this. I superimpose her high standards on my low ones, and soon I am digging out specks of wax I can hardly see or feel and scrubbing the glass until it sparkles. Halfway through I even revise my system, placing the candle holders in the second sink to drip dry instead of on the one towel Brother Isago has given me, which could easily become too wet to use.

When Shirley was in Stage Two of the Final Dive, in and out of ranting, she once complained that Julie and I took too long with her personal care. "What should we do?" we asked.

"Anticipate!" she snapped.

All the while I work, I think about Shirley. How, to her, cleaning was an art form and a passion. How Shirley had looked forward, when she retired, to giving her house a good cleaning and then cleaning our parents' house. I don't get it—the pleasure of cleaning. I am so uptight just doing the candle holders right that I hold my breath as I scrub. When I finish, I wipe down the sink, which I assume is a direct communication from Shirley, considering I've never thought to do it before, then wring out the towel and fold it over the faucet, carefully lining up the corners.

My second job is to polish all the wood in the church: the lecterns, the book stands, the chairs, the tabernacle. Brother Isago has given me furniture polish and an old sock, cut down and splayed like an animal skin on a pueblo dancer, and told me to "let it wick into the wood," whatever that means. I often watched Shirley polish furniture. She used Lemon Pledge and old cloth diapers. She loved the color and feel of mellowed wood.

With Shirley's spirit in me, I polish like a mad woman. I dig into corners and scrape off melted wax with my fingernails. I get onto my knees to do the base of the lectern, run my cloth over every curve, let the polish wick in. I give the tabernacle two coats even though I don't think I, a Catholic gone seriously AWOL, should be allowed to touch it. I close the doors of the triptych, framed in wood, and do the back side that nobody ever sees. Meanwhile, another guest works up a serious sweat sweeping the stone floor. He uses a heavy push broom and some special floor polishing stuff that looks like the red clay outside. In silence, we work like dogs.

We do not hum, like Shirley did while she cleaned.

With the sun blasting in through the huge windows, I get lost in the grain of each inch of wood that I polish. Later, I help the floor sweeper by using a smaller broom to dig into the corners, behind the three wood stoves, and between the rows of chairs. Then we make an executive decision and sweep out the sacristy, too, where the monks' robes hang on hooks. The job takes three hours, and by the end my back hurts— the resurrection of my old wicker shop injury. When my work partner goes outside to sweep the front step, I stand in the middle of the church, which gleams, floor and wood.

A job well done by me, I think.

Me and Shirley.

I am in and out of the church so many times between Friday and Sunday that my head is spinning like the child's in *The Exorcist*. No sooner do I start to grade the student papers I have brought along than the bell rings again, and I drop everything and sprint the quarter mile to the chapel. How do these nuns and monks get anything done, I wonder, what with charging back and forth to church all day long? And then I remember that church is precisely what they *are* doing.

On Sunday morning, when I wake up, it is snowing, just cranking up. I have read a warning in the information packet provided by Christ in the Desert: the red clay road quickly becomes impassable in inclement weather; if the weather is threatening, leave or face the possibility of being stranded. I go to the church, where a nun is building fires in the wood stoves and ask her if she thinks the weather looks bad enough to take off ahead of schedule. "It's hard to say," she answers, her cowboy boots dropping chunks of mud all over the floors we slaved on yesterday, "but it's probably better to leave while the road is still frozen, before the snow gets too deep."

I decide to go. I toss my down comforter (brought along in case the monks believed in thin blankets), my food stash, my Shirley candle, and my student papers into the trunk, scrape the snow off the windshield with my bare hands, turn on the ignition, and sit on my hands until they warm up. As I back out of the parking place, I hear the bells calling the faithful to church.

I have a strong intuition that I'm not going to get away with missing mass, a feeling so intense that I decide to turn around. Just as I make that decision, though, I hear a horrendous crack, and I slam on the brakes. I have hit something with my brand new car. I get out to look. Along the front passenger side are four long scrapes from rebar poles half buried in the dirt and snow. I run my fingers along the deep dents, like desert creeks waiting for rain, as the church bells chime a half mile away. Thanks a lot, God, I think, and then angrily I get back in the car and floor it. But I get only twenty feet because my front tire is blown. I climb out of the car again. Rubber hangs off the rim in a flap.

Once more, I dig the Owner's Manual out of the glove compartment. I find the jack and am working on the lug nuts when an older couple, fellow guests who call themselves Mom and Dad, comes along. They, too, are leaving early because of the snow. Dad changes the tire for me, something he says he has not done for twenty years, and then they lead the way to the highway, where they wave goodbye before heading north toward Colorado. I go south to the Abiquiu Inn for breakfast. The snow in my direction has already stopped, though to the north, where Mom and Dad are going, there is a surprise blizzard. I pray, as I have a second cup of coffee, they make it safely through the storm.

All through breakfast, all through the time I kill in Wal-Mart in Espanola while they replace my tire, I mentally accuse a wrathful Catholic God of punishing me unnecessarily harshly. I felt justified in leaving. The weather was terrible, after all. And I had done my part: cleaning the church, praying ten times a day, purchasing a Virgin of Guadalupe plaque from the gift shop, and being there among the monks, nuns, and Catholics for a whole weekend. It was a lot for me to do but I didn't do it right, and I got slammed.

The last time I heard that word was in May, right after I visited Shirley, right before her diagnosis was official. I went from Shirley's house to her son Billy's. I wanted to tell him in person to prepare himself, to expect the worst. "It's extra hard because nobody in the family has ever been really sick or died," I explained. "We don't know what to do. Think of it: my father is ninety-three. Nothing this terrible has happened to us in almost a century."

"And now we're going to get slammed," Billy said.

I choose the mountain route back to Albuquerque, from Los Alamos through Jemez Springs, where maybe I will teach next year. It is snowing like crazy up in the higher elevations. I can't even take my eyes off the road for a second to acknowledge the aftermath of the Los Alamos fires last summer. I inch along toward home.

When I get there, an e-mail from Shirley's buddy, Marcia, is waiting:

> While you're getting all spiritualed up, in silence, with the MONKS, I just welled up with such anger (AGAIN) at the thought of that Beautiful Woman, sitting up in bed, saying she was going to go to HELL!! What a religion!!! I'm still surprised "that priest" didn't say, OUT LOUD, "Marcia and Julie, you two are going to HELL!!!"

I laugh as I read it, but if you think about it, it's not really very funny.

Saturday

On Tuesday, a strange thing happened. I was loading the latest in a long line of broken vacuum cleaners into my car for a trip to the repair shop. Then I saw that Foncy, a many-decades-long friend of Julie Reichert's, was next door. She was supposed to leave for Oregon on the train the day before, but something went awry with the tracks east of here, and her train was delayed.

Foncy is a person I am getting to know slowly, usually in intervals of two to four hours, months or even years apart. We have had dinner at Garcia's Mexican Cafe, or sat under the mulberry tree in the yard in mis-matched chaise lounges, or been on hand for celebrations, like Julie Reichert's Fiftieth Birthday Bash—a milestone for her, considering the cancer that claimed her right breast at age forty-five. Foncy is gentle, delicate, and soft-spoken. She has pale skin, blue eyes, white hair, very white teeth. She reminds me of a particular painting by Vermeer in which a young Dutch woman in a white cap sits at a wooden table before a multi-paned window.

Sometimes I think I am too blustery for Foncy, too turbulent a spirit. But in January, right after I returned to New Mexico, I showed her one of my secret, secret photos of Shirley, though I never even mention these pictures to my closest friends. We had just had dinner together, and I talked non-stop about witnessing that Final Dive. Afterward, I felt compelled to provide a visual aid. Before Foncy's eyes, I pried the back off a picture frame, removed the black cardboard backing, and pulled out the little plastic baggie in which I keep these final snapshots of Shirley. I chose one and passed it to Foncy, who had never seen a pic-ture of my sister before. She held it very gently to her heart.

Three months later, this past Tuesday, when I saw that she was not on the train to Oregon after all, I spontaneously asked her if she would like to hear a chapter from my *Month of Sundays*. She said yes, so I aban-doned my vacuum cleaner and we went inside my *casita*. Foncy settled around the lumps in my couch while I found a readable copy of my True Vine chapter. I sat facing her in my adjustable desk chair and began to read.

Before I get to the end of the first paragraph, my throat closes and I start sobbing. Lately it's seemed that my tears are drying up, evaporating to form small, dark clouds that break into rain somewhere east of here, but suddenly I am in a cloudburst. I use the dishtowel that's laying on my desk to wipe my face, but I do not stop reading, and I don't even glance at Foncy. I can't. I just continue for fifteen straight minutes. Part way through, I notice that I've turned my chair and am now facing the corner.

When I finish, I make myself look up.

Foncy is crying, too. I toss her my dishtowel.

"Ain't that the saddest story you ever heard?" I say, aiming for levity. I stand up, just to move, just to do something, and Foncy stands up, and then we rush toward each other, throw our arms around each other, hug hard, no words.

One thing that touched me very deeply during Shirley's last months was her final hugs. When our sister Janet left for the last time (she had been east from Calgary three times), their last moment to see each other on earth, they hung on for dear life. Both their eyes were jammed tightly shut and still tears slipped out.

They held on.

And then they let go.

I cried too, standing in the doorway waiting to take Janet to the airport in Montréal for the emergency trip home, where her beloved husband John had had a heart attack. It was bad, so bad.

After a minute (a second? an hour?), Foncy and I separate.

Foncy is a massage therapist, tuned in to giving comfort.

And giving space.

"Isn't it weird about the True Vine? About it being closed?" I say as I collapse back into my desk chair.

"You get all ready, you open yourself up, and you get...nothing," Foncy answers, and we both laugh, loud and long.

Echoes of Angels
Albuquerque, NM

This Sunday, I pick the Echoes of Angels Church, located in a small shopping mall, amidst a T'ai-chi studio, a Chinese-Korean restaurant, an antique shop, a book bindery, and a beauty salon offering cheap make-up lessons. Shirley wore make-up every day: foundation cream, powder, lipstick, and mascara. All through her last summer, she carefully made up a healthier person, a woman with even skin tones and rosy cheeks. It took quite a while, every morning, and often she sent me to the drugstore for additional cosmetics. At night, when she wiped it off, she looked fifty years older. To me, it didn't seem worth it, all that effort, but Shirley believed in putting her best foot forward, no matter what the circumstances. It really wasn't vanity. She simply thought that being her best possible self was the right thing to do.

When I approach the door, I see that the Angels have posted a mission statement:

Our mission is to inspire, nurture, and be responsible for demonstrating Divine Love in our daily practice.

Like Shirley did, I think as I step inside. As so few people really do. I often wondered how she managed it: the formidable task of being so consistently loving and warm, so bright-spirited and caring. The only answer I ever came up with—that she was just born like that—tells me exactly nothing about the mystery of living love.

The room is small and, predictably, angels are the motif: angels trumpet on wall plaques and an angel is embroidered into the lace that covers the lectern. Angel statues stand on every horizontal surface while angel drawings and paintings hang from the vertical ones. One large angel, a doll in the "Good Witch" mode from the *Wizard of Oz*, mechanically moves its head and arms in a creepy manner. A handout explains that "Angels represent the Divine Ideas of the Creator that support and sustain our lives."

There are nine other people here, though by the end of the service, our numbers burgeon to thirteen, several of whom are ministers. Reverend Margie begins with a prayer which acknowledges the creator, the creation, and the creating; then we sing "Morning Has Broken"; finally, we recite the "Statement of Being":

God is all, both invisible and visible, One Presence, One Mind, One Power is all. This One that is all is perfect life, perfect love, and perfect substance. Man is the individualized expression of God and is ever one with this perfect life, perfect love, and perfect substance.

A different reverend leads us in a guided meditation, the theme of which is "Love Yourself," and the sermon is given by yet another minister, Reverend Nonie. Her theme is May Day, two days from now, which she refers to as Beltane, as the earth-based religions do. She talks interestingly about nature's cycle, which we all follow whether we admit it or not because we are part of nature. Autumn is equated with the release of the old (letting go), winter with withdrawal (a period of introspection, which she says is always "deep communion" with one's soul), spring with rebirth, and summer with abundance. She focuses mainly on endings and beginnings—about endings as loss and how we must meet the loss and move into the next beginning. "It is I who must begin," she says again and again, quoting someone whose name I do not catch. We begin anew in every second, and it is impossible to be lost, she says.

She follows up with a brief list of endings and beginnings in her life since the last Beltane. If I were doing the same for Shirley, I might say:

> May: Long, hot baths with nothing but Tylenol for pain.
> June: At last, a diagnosis. "It is I who must begin," Shirley
>   probably said to herself as she prepared to die.
> July - December: Dying and living. Living and dying.
>   Learning that when you are dying, you are living, right
>   up to the moment you are not.
> Christmas night: Letting go.
> May: Sometime, when the ground is thawed, burial.
>   Return to the earth.

We sing "Let There Be Peace on Earth," say a Unity Prayer, and snack on cookies and coffee. The service has lasted fifty minutes. I sit outside afterward on a wooden bench under a shade tree alive with psychedelic magenta blossoms. Twice, bird shit splatters near me, but I don't move. None hits me, even though I remain there a long time, experiencing a little bit of the abundant peace that is possible on this planet. I'm glad I came. It is I who must trust that somehow, some way, I'm hot on the trail of the spirit.

Friday

Last Sunday, late afternoon, Robert called me. He had been at my parents' for Sunday dinner and had heard—overheard, actually—that the day of Shirley's burial had been set. May 26th. Nine a.m. The Saturday of Memorial Day weekend.

"Did you know?" he asked.

"No," I sputtered. "It seems impossible that nobody would have told me."

It also seems incomprehensible that once the ground thaws, my sister Shirley, the light of my childhood and my lifelong friend, will be buried in it. She wanted a pine box, the cheapest casket made, the bottom of the casket line, but that was one more thing she did not get. Sometimes I get unruly images of Shirley's body in the funeral home vault awaiting burial with the random others who died when the snow was deep and the ground, rock hard.

When I hang up, I go hysterical.

I storm out the door to where Julie Reichert and Linda, Foncy's girlfriend, are sitting under the mulberry tree, which has just leafed out. In hot weather, it is ten degrees cooler under there. We often relax in its shade in plastic chaise lounges, cool drinks resting in the sand.

"The date is set for Shirley's burial," I announce, angrily.

"When?" Julie asks.

"After I get back east," I say. Then I shout, "I feel like shit!" and I run inside, slamming the door behind me. I throw myself on my bed for a formal breakdown. Of course, I have always known that Shirley's burial was coming, along with spring—the flowers, the leaves, the new beginning without her—and I thought I was prepared for it. I wrote her burial off as a cosmic punctuation mark, a period at the end of a sentence uttered six months ago, thoroughly comprehended on Christmas night at twenty after twelve. The burial was just a formality, I thought. The funeral and the memorial service were the closure.

I should have known better.

As an English teacher, I know full well the importance of final punctuation.

I turn over onto my back and watch clouds pass by the skylight. I spend hours in this position, observing the mobile Julie Reichert has made for me out of stones, sticks, and shells, which hangs from the skylight and is always in motion. No final resting place for it.

After a few days, when I am calmer, I call my niece Julie. Each time we speak, which is frequently, I ask her how she is, and she always responds, "I'm a total wreck." She is a total wreck because she has lost her mother. Predictably, she is a total wreck today. I ask her if there will be a priest graveside for Shirley.

"If we need one," I suggest, "maybe we could get Father Tom. He seems nice." After a pause, I add, "Better than the funeral priest."

"Anybody's better than him," says Julie.

"Jack the Ripper's better than him," I say.

We hang up. Two total wrecks.

Hillside Community Church
Albuquerque, NM

I am parked outside the Hillside Community Church a half hour before the service. Musicians arrive, remove guitars from their car trunks, and disappear into the plain white building whose parking lot is surrounded by a chain-link fence. Two potted desert plants sit next to a side door. They look dead, except for the blue plastic bag which is tangled up in one. It fills and deflates, like a lung in the easy breeze.

Yesterday, Paul Timmons, the faith healer, called me.

"I want to make sure I have the right person," he began. "Are you the woman who followed me..."

"Yes," I interrupted, "out into the parking lot after my sister Shirley's healing service at Notre Dame church in Malone." I carried the envelope full of money that he would not take. I said, "If you ever need a writer..." That was eight months ago, and yesterday he called. I jotted down the details of the writing job he needed done and promised immediate turn-around. I will happily do anything this man asks, even though, often, when I look back on Shirley's last months, I can't help but blame him for orchestrating her return to Catholicism, which made her doubt her own spirituality and carried with it the grim possibility of hell. Last fall, Shirley listened over and over to the tape I bought her of Paul reciting the rosary. At the end of every group of Hail Marys, he says a short little prayer that ends with "...and save me from the fires of hell." As Shirley fervently prayed in her bedroom, I, in the kitchen, would stop what I was doing, pretend to clap symbols together, and silently holler "Olé!" Save me from the fires of hell! Olé! Save me from the fires of hell! Olé! I do not believe in hell, or maybe, secretly, I believe in it too much.

We conversed for a few minutes before Paul asked, "Where do you go to church?"

"I'm not a Catholic, Paul," I answered, and after a beat, he said, "That's fine." Strangely, this was the second time within two hours that someone had asked me where I went to church. This morning at the post office my favorite clerk was on duty. As usual, I approached him saying, "Yo, Raaapheee" in an exaggerated New York accent. "Hey!" he replied. We did postal business, after which he asked if I'd lost weight. I have. Twenty pounds since I left the North Country, but only he and Julie Reichert have noticed.

"How'd you do it?" Raphy asked.

"No more junk food," I answered.

"That's good."

"The last of my evil ways," I sighed. "Now I'm waiting for the rapture." I said this because when I had my hair cut two days ago at Mr. Shears, a neighborhood barber shop full of Hispanic homeboys with tattoos, I listened to the barber, Ray, and another customer converse about a local woman. "She lost her mind when she got her master's degree," Ray said. "Now she's waiting for the rapture." "Oh yeah, the rapture," said the other guy, a huge man who arrived in a jacked-up truck. The sentence amused me, so for the fun of it I tried it out on Raphy. Like the man in the barber shop, he said, "Oh yeah, the rapture," and then he added, "What church do you go to?" "I don't," I said, because it seemed easier than saying every church, any church.

Then Paul asked me the same question.

Inside the Hillside Community Church a pianist is playing "As Time

Goes By" and other Happy Hour tunes. I notice that the music I hear in church generally makes me want to go to bars. I listen, relax, and remember.

May. Last May.

One year ago, I returned to the North Country on school vacation to see for myself what was up with Shirley. She picked me up at the airport in Burlington, Vermont, looking thin but beautiful. "Shirley! You don't look sick," I said with relief when I saw her. Shows what I knew. I drove her car home because she was too weak to do another three hours behind the wheel. She squirmed in her seat and arranged and rearranged her car pillow. (I have this pillow now.) The whole way back, I grilled her about pain, about eating, about body functions, and the next morning I made a list of questions for the doctor. She had made an appointment with a specialist in Burlington, and I had timed my visit east to go with her.

I was with Shirley every second of this visit, and this specialist never saw her. His assistant, a resident or intern, did. Later, the specialist blatantly lied, pretended to have met, evaluated, and treated my sister. But this is another bad doctor story which I do not want to remember. Not now, during church.

The night before her appointment with this specialist, though, when we still had high hopes for decent treatment, I slept at Shirley's. It was the first time I had stayed there in years. I took a bath while Shirley played the piano—the theme from the movie *Love Story*. I remembered the words and belted them out from the tub. "She fills my heart with very special things," I yelled, tears rolling down my cheeks. Later, when we met up in the kitchen, I said, "You've been practicing!" And she told me she'd been playing the piano intensively for six months to keep her mind off her pain. For six months, her doctor had not done one thing for her pain.

By the time I arrived back to stay in June, Shirley was a total wreck. Finally, she agreed to talk to Mary Lou about Hospice Care. The day we waited for Mary Lou to come, Shirley was doubled over in agony. She sat on the outside steps, white-faced, gripping her ankles. Impulsively, I placed my hands on her back. "Shirley," I said, "give me some of the pain. Give it up. Give it to me."

"I can't," she said. "I won't do it."

"I can take it. I'm strong. I weigh practically twice as much as you.

Give it to me," I insisted. Even I was shocked at the intensity in my voice.

Just then, Mary Lou arrived. She called Shirley's doctor and within a matter of hours we got the first morphine patch. Waiting for it in the drugstore, I remembered how, in an office visit with Shirley, I had asked her doctor what she thought of Hospice. This doctor replied, "I think they're a little too liberal with pain medication." In the drugstore, remembering this, I said, "Fucking asshole" right out loud.

I am so lost in these memories that when I come back, I realize I am still hearing *Love Story* instead of what the pianist is playing.

There are about fifty people in the congregation for the opening prayer. At least ten are alone, like I am. In most churches, I am the only one who is alone, or one of the few. The prayer is short, the gist being, Let me accept a new freedom and new joy. "And so it is," it ends. This is followed by a classical piece performed by the Hillside Flute Duo. The music evokes images of Greece, shepherds, the pastoral life. I watch the flutists, a woman and man, breathe. They gulp air, then portion it out to make music. But today, the little gasps remind me of Shirley gasping, little gasps for breath, in the very last moments of her life. A song which was ending. I still hear Julie saying, "Don't panic, Mom. You're all right. You don't have to breathe anymore. Everything is all right." And it was. If everything can be all right at a moment like that, a dying moment, then why is living so hard? I want to solve this basic mystery, but before I can get started Dr. Larry Morris, the head honcho, steps to the microphone for his sermon, "Doorway to Beauty," and begins to toss out jokes, like confetti:

> Beauty is in the mind of the bar holder.
> I almost had an affair with a psychic but she left me before
>   we met.
> Black holes are where God divides by zero.
> Why didn't the skeleton cross the road? Because he didn't
>   have the guts.
> I married Miss Right. I just didn't know her middle name
>   was Always.
> I still miss my ex, but my aim's improving.
> God give me the senility to forget the people I never liked.

He reads poetry by William Carlos Williams, e.e. cummings, and James Wright and then segues into his sermon. Beauty, he says, is only noticed in the absence of self. And complete appreciation of beauty, without consciousness of the self, makes it come more often. "Don't hold back because you're waiting for a better time to reveal your beauty and your gifts to the world," he advises. "Give yourself to beauty. That is God in you." He tells us that we are in the entry portal to an experience that can take us beyond anywhere we've been up to now. Any minute, we can have spiritual ecstasy. Periodically, he tells more jokes, one about a traveling Sufi and a meatball vendor, which gets us howling. When we begin our meditation, I breathe in beauty.

During the final hymn, "Let There Be Peace on Earth," I start to cry and cannot sing the line, "Let me walk with my family" because I have thought so much this past week about not walking with my sister Shirley ever again.

About burying her, deep in the cold, cold earth.

Friday

Of course, having done his small writing job, I have been thinking about Paul. And Shirley. About how unpredictable it is who will step in, or simply appear, to change the course of a person's life. It is magic, I know. Last summer, one afternoon, I told Shirley the story of Leroy Begay, the Navajo elder who showed up in my UNM office and ended up restructuring me, I'm pretty sure, on the cellular level. I told her how my ribs began to shake as I listened to him, as if something very important were shaking loose, shaking free.

Shirley, sitting in her Mother's Day chair covered with Marcia's afghan, listened to me the way she always did: with complete attention. She listened with her ears, eyes, and hands as I began.

Leroy told me he was seriously drunk, totally plastered, for thirty-five years. *Thirty-five years!* He slept in gutters and begged for food. And then, one day out on the Navajo rez, when he opened his eyes after having passed out in the dirt as usual, he saw a little bird singing in the piñon tree. His cheek pressed into the filth, hardly able to move, his mind suddenly cleared: That bird is singing his heart out and I am killing myself, he thought. And I am a member of the bird clan.

It was hard, almost impossible at times, but Leroy never had another drink, from that day to this. "Everybody has an assignment," he told me. "I got mine that day." Now, doing his assignment, he attends UNM in pursuit of a college degree in fine arts, so he can return to the rez and teach elementary school.

"Leroy was my bird in the piñon tree," I said to Shirley.

I didn't have to tell her that it all boiled down to the mysterious force called grace, which Leroy taught me is available to anyone. No matter where you've been or what you've done, it's ready and waiting to pour in and wake you up. I think you have to be momentarily undefended, free of your ego, and without agenda or expectation. Then, given the right conduit (for me, it was Leroy), it floods in and, in a split second, blasts opens the door of your prison. Leroy's dark prison was alcohol. And mine was severe emotional pain brought on by the idea that I was unlovable and therefore unloved.

This is what I believe, what I know: once you wake up in this way, you might fall asleep again, you might drift, snooze, slumber, dream, but you cannot go unconscious. You cannot totally forget what you've experienced in your own cells: the light and the truth. It's right there in your blood, forever after, a reference point, as sure and as solid as North on a compass. I know this because my own deepest despair got unhitched from me that day. Like the last car of a long train, it got unhooked, and I went on without it. And the farther I get away from it, the more useless it all seems in retrospect.

"How did he penetrate into your heart so deeply?" my sister whispered.

"I guess I was ready." Then I added the one and only Shakespeare quote I find useful on a day-to-day basis: "The readiness is all."

Shirley was ready for Paul.

He arrived out of nowhere, and I think he became the most important person in her life at the end. Today, I am remembering three particular moments, all of which took place during the Final Dive:

Moment One: It is Tuesday, December 12th. Shirley is in Stage One. The night before last, she signed over her car to me. Yesterday, she fell backwards on the bed and then said she was never getting up again. She made goodbye calls to her kids. Today, she called each of her sisters and we pre-arranged a time for her to speak to our parents on their two extension phones. Laurie held the phone for Shirley while she thanked her parents, our parents, for everything, including life itself, and said goodbye. She hung up, a total wreck. One second later, the phone rang. It was Paul. Shirley told him she was ready for God to come and get her. They prayed together that her passing over would be easy and that she would see Jesus in heaven. When she hung up, she was beaming.

Moment Two: Days had gone by. Shirley was slipping away but not fast enough. In her delirium, she ranted: "Why doesn't God want me?" or "God doesn't want me" or "I have to burn more" or "Purgatory is O.K." In a clear moment, she asked her son Jimmy to call Paul because she needed to clarify something important. Jimmy left a message on Paul's 800 number.

When Paul called back, I held the phone for Shirley. She could barely speak, and he could barely hear her. She said, and it took a long time, that she thought she had phrased it wrong when they had prayed, and that was why she couldn't move along, out of life. She had said God could come to get her, but she meant to say, "I will go to God. He doesn't have to come get me." She stopped talking. I wondered what was happening, if Paul was still on the line with her, so I propped the phone to her ear with a pillow and ran to the kitchen extension. I lifted the receiver and listened. In a soothing voice, Paul was saying, "When you get to heaven, Shirley, would you do me a favor? Would you ask Jesus to keep me healthy so I can continue to do His work, here on earth? When you stand in front of Jesus, could you do that for me?" he asked, and she whispered yes. Then she was silent. "Shirley?" Paul said in his gentle voice, "Shirley?"

I peeked into Shirley's room. The phone had fallen away from her face. "She's sleeping," I think I said. "This is her sister."

"How much time do you think she has left?" Paul asked.

"Not much. A few days." (She had twelve.)

"Will you call me if she needs me?"

"I will."

Moment Three: Shirley is deep, deep into Stage Two. Julie and I are standing at her bedside. Suddenly, she tries to raise her hands. She is so weak that they fall down onto her chest or collapse backward onto the pillow. She keeps trying until she gets them up, clasped into the prayer position. "I stand before you, Jesus," she says. "I am asking you please…" Each word is a monumental effort, and her hands shake like she has advanced palsy. Julie and I stand, breathless, and watch. "…please, to keep Paul wealthy. No, not wealthy. That's not right. Keep Paul healthy so he can do your work here on earth. I ask you this, Jesus, now, when I'm standing before you."

"Do you think she's really there?" Julie and I whisper to each other; "and if so, hey, what about us? We could use a little assistance here, too."

But she only mentions Paul before her boney, blotchy hands fall down onto the bed above her shoulders and she cannot raise them up, ever again. I think but I'm not sure that those were her last words. I wish I could remember this exactly, but I can't.

When I spoke to Paul a few days ago, he said he thought Shirley had been healed that day in September at Notre Dame church. "When she got up out of that wheelchair, I thought…" he said, but he didn't continue. "I don't question it anymore. I used to, but now I just accept it all as the will of God," he finished.

I remember the way Paul anoints his hands with holy oil and lays them on the sick. The way he travels to Catholic churches encouraging people to seek forgiveness through confession. How he sent Father Tom to Shirley. How Father Tom provided the easiest five minutes of Shirley's life.

But I'm also convinced that my sister would not have even thought of hell—it would not have crossed her mind once at the end—if Paul had not brought her back into the Catholic church. Thinking this, I get furious at him. Then I remember that day on the porch steps when all I wanted in the world was to have healing hands, and I admit I'm probably just jealous of Paul who, after all, is doing his assignment.

I know I was doing my assignment when I returned to the North Country to take care of Shirley. And I also know that I probably couldn't have—or wouldn't have—gone if Leroy hadn't arrived (just as Shirley got sick, too) to shake loose some atrophied part of me. If he hadn't arrived to remind me how uncomplicated life can be if you let it.

A long time after Shirley died, my sister Mary told me a true story. Once, during Shirley's last summer, when she and Shirley were alone, Mary asked Shirley why she thought I'd come east to take care of her.

Shirley said, "I think I'm her bird in the piñon tree."

Mary was understandably perplexed. "What does that mean?"

"Ask Julie," Shirley said.

I often wonder about this. Clearly, Shirley thought that part of her assignment was to wake me up in some crucial way. But I don't feel awake when I wonder about it. I feel dreamy, slow, and dull. I wish I could ask her what she meant, what song she felt she was singing, whether she thought I opened my heart and heard it.

Sometimes Leroy and Shirley fly together in my dreams, a couple of beautiful birds in search of the nearest piñon tree.

Emmanuel Metropolitan Community Church
Albuquerque, NM

In a few days, I will head to the North Country for the summer, and I dread returning to the place where I took such a severe beating. I am barely back on my feet, and I know I'm bound to get knocked down, flattened, if I go back there. But my parents need help, and the ties that bind my marriage are so seriously frayed, they could easily snap once and for all. I often wonder if all marriages endure such parched spells, when the emotional gap perilously widens and the what-for-anyway questions build. When Robert and I were married, late thirties for me and forty for him, we had both chiseled our criteria for a spouse to the same, odd quality: someone who can leave me alone. There are many benefits to such an eccentric union. Freedom, for one. But the downside is that you often feel alone. You often are. And sometimes you have to scramble mightily to reconnect.

So I'm going.

I feel depressed and helpless when I imagine the Sundays I will spend in the Christian churches of the North Country. No one will mention Beltane or tell jokes from the pulpit. No one will play "As Time Goes By" as a warm-up act. Instead, I'll be beating my breast and pleading guilty, guilty, guilty to unspecified charges.

To offset this worry, I place a call to Alexcia, my friend and acupuncturist. "Do you know any non-Christian churches?" I ask, and she says she knows a guy who goes in for pagan rites. "Pagans are good," I say. She offers to call him for me. This leads me to a nondescript building in a nondescript neighborhood. The sign in front says, "Come as you are believing as you do." It is raining when I leave the car. Inside the church, I am greeted by two women, both very masculine, and led into the church which has wall hangings of the red AIDS awareness ribbon, a painting of the Holy Spirit in the form of a dove, and a giant cross constructed of distressed wood with a multi-colored quilt draped over the crosspiece. To one side, a trio (voice, guitar, and ukulele) practice, and the female minister, Reverend Pat, wearing an off-white monk's robe, prepares the altar. The stole around her neck is embroidered on one end with a steaming loaf of bread; on the other end is a goblet into which grapes are piled. Several women, noticeably butch, come over to shake my hand. The few men in the room are far less masculine than these women.

I begin to peruse the program and come upon this statement:

> Emmanuel Metropolitan Community Church members and
> friends are lesbian, heterosexual, gay, bisexual, and trans-
> gendered. We are on many spiritual paths.
> We are old and we are young. We are many colors. We are
> making a difference.

I look around again. In graduate school, we might label this group "historically underrepresented" or "marginalized." No doubt, some of these non-mainstream people have been pushed away from other churches. But here they are, I think, and here I am. I open the looseleaf binder I've been given and read the church's mission statement:

> Emmanuel Metropolitan Community Church has been
> called out to be an inclusive community of worship. We
> seek to develop, within a Christian context, a closer and
> more meaningful relationship with the God of our under-

standing, to create a supportive community of faith and action, and to provide opportunities for the church body to act as the hands and feet of Christ in corporal acts of mercy and justice.

Not pagan after all.

The service begins. Reverend Pat says, "Happy Mother's Day to all, including the feminine side of our guys." In my general busyness, I have forgotten Mother's Day, and I remind myself to call my own mother later. I think of Shirley's kids and experience a stab of sadness. Their first Mother's Day with no mother to call.

As usual, there are songs, announcements, and handholding. We pray for the wisdom to save the earth, restore the water, refresh the air. The responses vary from "Amen" (Judeo-Christian), to "Ashe" (African), "Aho" (Indian), and "So mote it be" (Wicca). At sermon time, Grandmother Tommie, a black woman who moves slowly and seems much older than the fifty-eight she claims, settles into the rocking chair at the front of the room and begins to talk about motherhood. Like Shirley, she raised six children, though only half of them were hers. She warns us not be to too quick to judge our mother because we can never know what it was like to walk in her shoes. "God couldn't be everywhere every minute," she says, "so he placed some blessed women on earth to spread his love. And he called them mothers." And women who mother, she reminds us, are not always the same ones who give birth. I think about Shirley, who mothered me.

Grandmother Tommie says that it was a tradition in her family to purchase red carnations on Mother's Day. Each one in the family wore one in honor of their mother. This went on from 1944 to 1979 when her grandmother died. Then, for the first time, a white carnation appeared among the red flowers, which became the new tradition.

No sooner does she finish speaking than Reverend Pat passes around a tray of decorated votive candles. There are red ones, like the red carnations, to take if we have a living mother. "But if someone who mothered you has died in the last year," Reverend Pat says, "take a white one." I am sobbing as I lift a white candle with a green ribbon off the tray. Reverend Pat gives thanks, on our behalf, for the mothers we had or the mothers we wish we had, and she advises us to learn to mother ourselves.

Here, communion is open to all. "You don't have to be a member of this or any other church," says Reverend Pat. We even have options: communion can be given by the pastor or taken out of a chalice privately on another part of the altar; we can be anointed with oil or receive a prayer, a hug, or nothing at all.

I choose nothing, partly because I cannot regain control of myself. I hold my little white candle in a clenched fist as tears cascade down my cheeks. I watch others go forward to the altar: a young black man with an old-fashioned Afro stands alone in the private communion area; a white man, probably in his fifties, helps his mother negotiate her walker to the front to receive a hug from Reverend Pat. Afterward, we beg forgiveness for polluting Mother Earth. And then we sing one final hymn:

Our God is not a woman, our God is not a man.
Our God is both and neither, our God is who I am.
From all the roles that bind us, Our God has set us free.
What freedom does God give us? The freedom just to be.

Grandmother Tommie has created a huge Mother's Day card on poster board. We are invited, if we so choose, to write our mother's name on it. I stand in line for this.

I write: Shirley Carter. Strong and beautiful in life and at the moment of her death.

Then I run to my car.

Rap music blasts from a second-floor apartment across the street. I put my white candle in the cup holder and collapse over the steering wheel as if I've been shot. I cry for a long, long time.

Saturday

The formerly snow-white North Country is now intensely green and full of mosquitoes, black flies, pouring rain, grey skies, and memories of Shirley. My mother, gazing out at her lawn two days ago, said, "Look at those violets. The whole field is purple. If Shirley were here..." And then, as she does many times per day, she teared up and turned her head away. Shirley loved spring. All the seasons, really. She would pull to the side of the road, overcome by beauty, get out of her car, and just stand there. Her gaze was like water which dripped everywhere. I think in its way it nourished the wild flowers, the tall grass, the hardwood trees.

Next week, a week from today, Shirley will be buried in the earth she loved. I asked my father, who lives in his reclining chair now with oxygen strapped to his face, if he wanted to attend her burial. "We can get you there," I said. "We can get portable oxygen and take you in a wheelchair."

"I haven't been out of the house since November," he said—fearfully, I thought.

"That doesn't mean you can't go," I said and then added, "Maybe you'd like to say something about Shirley at her burial."

And my father, who never shuts up, who tells the same ninety-four years' worth of stories over and over again, goes suddenly silent. I look up from my lap. His constant monologue, usually about guys he beat up, insulted, or taught a good lesson to, is even more obvious in its rare absence. Then he says, softly, "Oh, I don't want to say anything. I'm… I'm… I'm spellbound."

I slump back, into the couch.

My father speechless? This is a first.

Later, I tell this story to my sisters. Laurie just looks at the floor. When I re-tell it to Mary on the phone, silence pulsates. When Robert comes home from work, I tell him as he changes his clothes, and he says nothing. We are all spellbound. I wonder why I, like my father, feel a need to tell this same story again and again to anyone who will listen. Maybe I'm trying to take the starch out of it, as my mother would say.

Later my father quietly informs me that he has spent the whole winter in his reclining chair—morning, noon, and night—pondering why Shirley lasted so long and suffered so much. "It was God's way of teaching us a lesson," he announces. "By the time she passed on, there wasn't one person who wasn't ready and willing to let her go."

Why won't God let you go, I am thinking, though I don't say it. For years, whenever anyone asked him how he was, he said, "I'm heading for the bone-yard," or "I'm just waiting for the Good Lord to take me," or "If something happens to me, Mother will be taken care of." Every day now he says, "I wish I could get out of this mess," and he makes a sweeping gesture that includes the reclining chair, the oxygen, the commode placed in the TV room next to his recliner. "I can't do a damn thing anymore," he gripes. When he asks, "What's the point?" I certainly have no answer.

When Shirley was in Stage Two of the Final Dive, she felt the same way. "I want to go to God," she said, over and over. Her daughter, Julie, whispered, "It's not your time yet, Mom." "I want to go to God," Shirley repeated. "I want to go to God."

During this phase, her son Johnny wildly paced the house. At every step, he pretended to karate chop whatever was in front of him: furniture, windows, doorjambs, people. "Pssshhht!" he would hiss as he threw his punches. It was catching. Soon, Julie and I were adding, "Nyyeettt! Nyyeett!" and pretending to poke each other's eyes out, like the Three Stooges.

The day before Shirley took the Final Dive was the day that Johnny called to tell her that he had finally asked his girlfriend, Barbara, to marry him. Shirley was thrilled. Everyone was. We all want Johnny to be happy, and since he met Barb he's happier than he's ever been. I think, if I remember right, that first he told Shirley he was engaged and later in the conversation she told him it was time now for her to say goodbye. She knew the end was very close. "This is it," she told me, steadily, after she hung up with John. Then she called the rest of her kids.

Johnny arrived within a few days, but by then his mother was no longer coherent. It was a terrible time. Billy, Julie, Johnny, Jim, and I were there. Kimberly had just left. Neal was coming. We gathered in the living room to discuss whether we should give Shirley her fast-acting "breakthrough" (extra morphine for pain that the morphine patches were not handling) on a three-hour schedule, or wait until she showed a sign of distress. Julie did not want to overmedicate her when there was a slim, slim hope that she might wish to communicate something when she "came up." On the other hand, nobody wanted her to be in any pain at all, and we were not certain we could tell when she needed relief.

Afterward, when I was in Shirley's room, she suddenly asked for Johnny.

"Shirley is asking for you!" somebody, maybe me, said, and Johnny rushed into her room. She had not specifically acknowledged his presence since he had arrived. She was already very far away.

She looked right at him and said, clear as a bell, "Tell them to give me my stinking breakthrough." And then she was gone again.

Later, Johnny came out of her room into the kitchen. "I thought she was going to say something about my engagement," he said, and I could tell he was not sure whether to laugh or cry. I started to laugh. "Tell them to give me my stinking breakthrough," I repeated, which sounded like the funniest line I'd ever heard in my life.

I still laugh sometimes when I think of it: its unexpectedness, the strange moment of clarity, the use of the word "stinking." But other times, I can't help but wonder how Shirley, two rooms away, heard our discussion. We thought she was essentially gone. Now I wonder if people in that state are essentially everywhere.

First Christian Church
Brushton, NY

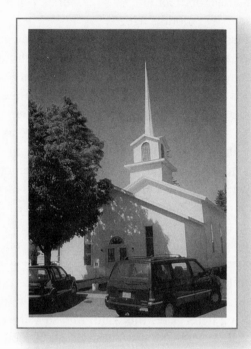

I am parked in Shirley's car outside the First Christian Church in Brushton, New York, and I am nervous. This is the church we fled to after Shirley's dreary funeral mass to celebrate her life with music, food, and fellowship. We needed a place to laugh and cry, and there was no room for that in the Catholic church, at least not according to Shirley's funeral priest. Mary Lou, her beloved Hospice nurse, made arrangements with her minister, and we flocked here, taking over the kitchen, dining room, and church.

I am anxious because I know that the Golden Age—my sixteen Sundays in Albuquerque—is over. I stepped lively through them, but now I am at the portal of the Dark Age. It's not this church that makes me feel this way. The church is as I remember it: simple, clean, and lovely. There is a faux window in front with a painting of an Adirondack scene: green grass, blue lake, rounded mountain in the distance. There is no hanging, bleeding, stabbed, suffering, dying Jesus anywhere in sight. The door to the dining hall is open and people are slowly moving from there into the church. Some carry Styrofoam coffee cups, as I did when I came into this room for Shirley's memorial. I sit in the same pew I sat in on that day five months ago.

By coming east, I know, I have taken the lid off my grief. I have left my busy and distracting life and entered one in which I will do nothing but stand by as my father declines. The sweet diversity of the churches of New Mexico is gone, and so is my anonymity. Here, in the North Country, everyone knows everyone's business. Here in the North Country, I will be scraped raw. And Shirley is not here to talk to.

Since I arrived, I have been basically prone on the porch swing. There is so much to avoid, so much to hide, so many emotions to ignore, and somehow I know, deep inside, it is inevitable that I will have to face it all. I try to arm myself, knowing that in my recovery from my sister's death, I have just taken a turn for the worse.

I watch a little girl in the pew in front of me toss a ball painted like a bloody eyeball up and down, up and down, as a young man welcomes us. "Is that the minister?" I whisper to the man seated in front of me. This man has already asked me where I'm from, who my parents are, and what I'm doing here. "He's the youth minister," he answers. "He's from Mississippi. That's why he sounds so funny." An outsider, like me. People notice outsiders. The minister's wife has introduced herself, and I feel many pairs of eyes on me. But this abruptly ceases when the praying, singing, and scripture reading start. We sing "Tell It to Jesus" but my memory traces provide an alternate soundtrack: Joan Baez, Sarah MacLachlan, Andrea Bocelli, Iz K. The music we played at Shirley's memorial service.

The children are called to the front for their lesson. The youth minister tells the story of a little girl whose mother is extremely sick in the hospital. The nurse comes to take the mother's temperature, and the girl wanders to the window where she spies a rainbow. "Who made the rainbow?" he asks the kids.

"God!" they holler on cue.

"And the little girl thought, If God can make a rainbow, he can make my mother better. And that's called faith."

But what if Mommy dies, I almost shout. I am impatient with the notion of faith healing. Long ago, as Shirley died, I became skeptical of any notion of control over death. "She'll go when she's ready. She can pick her time," several people confidently announced.

"That's total crap—just a romantic notion," I snapped back. "There's nothing going on here but an endurance test. For Shirley and everyone else, it's about endurance, and that's *it*." This is what I learned. Would it surprise the kids gathered around the youth minister?

It sure surprised me.

The pastor, Dr. David Roberts, is dressed in a suit with a white shirt and tie and plays the trumpet during the hymns. His sermon, "Overcoming Prayerlessness," goes on for a good hour. He loves to categorize and list, and actually, I do, too. Pastor Roberts has many reasons why believers should listen for and to God:

1) God wants to communicate
2) a saving relationship includes fellowship with God
3) God the Father desires to guide the believer
4) listening and praying is an integral part of the relationship between the believer and Jesus Christ.

But how does God speak? In two ways:

1) through the Bible, and
2) through the direct leading of the Holy Spirit.

Way Number Two is further subdivided into four categories. I drift away, stay gone until it's time to leave. Pastor Roberts is out front shaking hands. When I step up to him, I blurt out, "My sister died in December."

He looks at me carefully.

"You let us have her memorial service here."

"Oh…yes. I remember."

"Thank you, thank you," I say as I vigorously pump his hand. "Thank you."

Then I hurry to the 7-11 on the corner and buy a bag of jelly beans. I eat them by the handful in Shirley's car. Like the lilacs, they fill the car with a sweet, syrupy smell. All around me, flowers are bursting forth like fireworks.

I imagine that Shirley's flowers are up by now.

Six more days until she's buried.

I fight the urge to make a long list of the ways in which I miss my sister.

Saturday

Today we buried Shirley. It was overcast with occasional drops of rain. The burial was set for nine, but Robert and I arrived early, after a pit-stop in the fresh flower department of Price Chopper, where I bought two bunches of daisies, Shirley's favorite flower. I put one bunch in a jelly jar with water, and the other one I broke apart and gave to people. We huddled together as the cars pulled in: all Shirley's kids, their kids, our mother, all our sisters except Janet, who could not come from Calgary, our husbands, our aunts, Shirley's friends, her admirers.

Everyone was there but the priest.

The group grew and we milled around, as if we were at some surreal cocktail party. Shirley's coffin—her name hand printed on a white stick-on label on the end—waited under a canopy. People stayed away from it. Shirley's marker, not in the ground yet, sat off to the side, engraved with just-the-facts:

Shirley Kress Carter
February 20, 1937 - December 26, 2000

Our eyes are red. I see such pain in my nephew Johnny's that I don't know what to do. Or say. I mill on.

And still Father Tom does not show. He made her confession the easiest five minutes of her life, but now he is five minutes late for her burial, and it's not easy for anyone.

I hear a man introduce himself to my brother-in-law. Twenty years ago, while visiting Shirley, I met this man in her kitchen. They had been seeing each other, which meant sitting in the living room holding hands, for several months and were thinking of getting married. Last summer, I asked Shirley about this, and she told me that when she was ready, he wasn't, and vice versa.

"She probably told him to dry up and blow away," my niece Julie commented when I told her. "She said that all the time." I remember that. Dry up and blow away.

Like Shirley is, right now.

When Shirley was descending into Stage Two of the Final Dive, I was sitting with her in her little bedroom while she rambled in hallucinatory fragments about her real or imaginary life. For me, it was like being trapped in a dream: some of what she said made sense, but then some incongruous series of details would emerge, and I would be lost. Patiently, I tried to piece together the parts I didn't know about, as if it were my job to arrange her random ranting into an accurate linear sequence.

"When was this?" I would ask. She was agitated about some event in which a person who came into her life "for a little while," she said, had fooled her, sworn her to secrecy, and lied about something related to two children for whom she was not responsible. Over and over, she cried, "I gave him my word."

"Shirley," I said, hoping to comfort her, "if you broke your word, it's O.K."

"I didn't break my word," she snapped.

"It would be O.K. if you did," I repeated, groping my way along this conversation.

"It's never O.K. to break your word," she corrected me. Then, right in the middle of this, she switched memory tracks and said, "I loved Jack…a little."

"Do you want me to call him, Shirley?"

"No, no," she said, impatiently. "He died." And then she switched again, back into the story of the two children I had never heard of whom she wanted to protect, though they were not her responsibility. More about not breaking her word.

After she passed, I felt compelled to tell this man that my sister had said she loved him but I couldn't find him in the phone book, and then I left the North Country. Later I got an e-mail from Marcia, who said he had called her, though she had never met him, wildly upset about Shirley. He hadn't known Shirley was sick until he saw her obituary in the paper, he said. That obituary had thrown him for a loop. He even showed up at my parents' to shed alligator tears (as my mother put it) for Shirley.

The night that Shirley signed her car over to me, while I was searching for the title, I came across three bundles of poems and (I think) love letters. I started to kid her about her secret life, opened one poem, and began to read it out loud. "Shhh!" she said. "Throw them away, all of them." Her tone and energy surprised me, and I looked up from the pile of envelopes in my lap. Her eyes, more yellow than brown, were dead serious, so I immediately dumped the whole pile in her waste basket and soon after transferred them to the garbage can outside. I resisted my every urge to dig them out again and read them. I consider this to be one of my greatest moments of self control in life, and I'm surprised I did it. So is everyone else. But they weren't there to hear that "Shhh!" or see the pleading look in Shirley's eyes.

Looking back, I'm pretty sure that the search for the title to the car was a ruse to get me into the drawer where the letters were because the second I threw them away, Shirley said, "You know what? I think the title's in the metal box under my bed."

I do not know if any of those letters or poems came from Jack when I ask him to step to one side with me. We stand on my grandmother's grave.

And still the priest does not come. It is well after nine.

"I wanted to tell you that near the end," I say to Jack, "Shirley said she loved you." He nods once and that is all. "I didn't know she was sick," he says, as if he still cannot believe it, no matter how many people he tells. "I found out about her death in the paper." After a beat he repeats the sentence again, a broken record. I move my foot off my grandmother's marker.

"Did she ask for me?" I see the need in his eyes and am tempted to lie, but I don't.

"She didn't ask for anybody," I say. I do not add that when I asked her if she wanted me to call him, she said, "He died."

There is nothing more to say, and we both melt back into the crowd. I stand with Marcia and Robert and watch my mother stare at Shirley's coffin. My mother wears a purple blazer, which Shirley bought for her, and a flowered skirt, which Shirley also bought for her. My sister Mary and I wear matching sweaters that Shirley knit.

Father Tom's phone is busy, so the funeral director tears off to the rectory. Nervously, we check out every car that turns into the cemetery, of which there are many. Finally, forty-five minutes late, Father Tom shows up. He wears black trousers, black shirt, Birkenstock sandals. There is something yellow (probably eggs) stuck in his beard. He says to the assembled group, "I usually sleep late on Saturday, and that's what I did. I forgot. I'm sorry." In a way, I admire his honesty. It must be terribly tempting to tell a whopper at a time like this. I can think of three off the top of my head: 1) A person in crisis showed up at my door. 2) I had to rush to the hospital to give the last rites. 3) I was lost in prayer. "I didn't even think to look at my palm pilot," he adds as he moves toward Shirley's coffin.

The service is short and focused on resurrection.

I have asked Marcia to read a poem. Last summer she often read poetry to Shirley, and once when she started to read this very poem, Shirley joined in, from memory. It is from "Song of Myself" by Walt Whitman:

> I bequeath myself to the dirt to grow from the grass I love
> If you want me again, look for me under your bootsoles.
> You will hardly know who I am or what I mean
> But I shall be good health to you nevertheless
> And filter and fiber your blood.
> Failing to fetch me at first sight, keep encouraged
> Missing me one place, search another
> I stop somewhere waiting for you.

Julie and Kimberly almost shout with grief at the first line, and I worry that I have made a mistake asking Marcia to read it. Afterward, though, they both say it was perfect. And then Neal speaks about his mother. He says many lovely things, but I particularly remember this: "She liked to fix things, and she was good at it—whether it was clothes, or furniture, or broken hearts."

Shirley helped mend my broken heart, broken spirit, broken self. When I was young, it was a full-time job for her. It feels so funny now to be strong and healthy while she, my foundation person, is being buried in the damp earth.

When it is over, Jack gives my niece Julie a large envelope. Inside is a gorgeous picture of Shirley.

We gather in a circle around it.

"Shirley!" I cry, loud and silent, from deep inside.

"Shirley!" I cried when I was alone in her house for a rare moment after she died and found myself running from room to room, looking for her.

Shirley.

Church of
Jesus Christ of the Latter Day Saints
Malone, NY

I have a dream that I am sitting in a candlelit place while my waist-length hair is being braided by an unknown person. In the dream, my hair is full of life, light, and body. As each section is tamed into its place in the braid, I am enormously relieved. I wake up thinking that my grief, like my hair, needs to get organized, patted into place. Secretly, I feel myself edging my way toward one simple, sickening truth: I did not come east last year to take care of Shirley out of love; I came in response to the loss of it, the big blank that siphoned out the love. I desperately need to re-enter those blank years between me and Shirley, maybe braid them in. But the truth is, I never allow myself to face them or even admit they exist. But now I know, I feel it in my gut, that I, like Shirley, have to take the Final Dive straight into that blankness if I'm going to move along into my next life.

"I'm just not in the group anymore!" I once wailed to Shirley, probably when I was forty and feeling more like a five-year-old. "I'm left out!"

"There is no group," she emphatically responded. That was in the blank years, but it is too soon to braid it in. My heart pounding, I jot down this random memory on a credit card receipt. As I wait in the parking lot of the Church of the Latter Day Saints, I stare at it as if it's written in Chinese ideograms.

The Mormons meet in the building formerly occupied by the Great Northern Jeep/Eagle dealership. The last time I was in this parking lot, maybe eight years ago, I was dreaming of buying a used Jeep that I could not afford. I have come here to meet Neal, the one and only churchgoer in Shirley's family. On my way, I detoured past the cemetery where Shirley is. The flowers are already wilting on my sister's grave.

Listlessly, I enter the former showroom. I find Neal, and we sit together in the midst of the folding chairs. The music from the small portable organ is periodically drowned out by the traffic zooming along Route 11 just outside the display windows. I feel somewhat impenetrable—locked inside myself with memories that have just begun to appear like magic writing on random scraps of paper. As a distraction, I stare at an image of Jesus Christ on the front wall. This Jesus is darker by far than anyone in this room. He looks immensely worried, angry, and tense. "That's the most stressed-out Jesus I've ever seen," I whisper to Neal. "He has a lot to be stressed out about," says Neal.

I was a stressed-out child, though I did not appear to be. "Everybody thought you were happy-go-lucky," Shirley said, and she told me a story to prove it:

> Once you were climbing up on that high wall in front of
> our house at West Point and jumping off and Dad told you
> to stop. "You're going to hurt yourself jumping off there!"
> he said, but you ignored him. Later, when you came in cry-
> ing with a bloody knee, he said, "See? I told you you would
> get hurt jumping off that wall." "Oh shut up, Daddy,"
> Shirley said I said. "I didn't hurt myself jumping off. I hurt
> myself climbing up." Shirley said my father's face twitched
> to keep from laughing while my older sisters held their
> breath on my behalf. No one spoke to my father that way.
> "She's the only normal kid we've got," he said quietly to
> my mother, according to Shirley.

My father taught me, expected me, to be tough, to follow my own strong will and not to apologize for it, and I did. But secretly, I locked myself in the closet and cried so hard I could not breathe. Waves of deep, mysterious sadness washed through me, washed me away, and I was emotionally bereft, lonely, scared of everything. That was when Shirley would whisper through the door that she wanted to come in. I would crawl onto her lap and drink in her silence. I can still feel her arms around me. She never asked for an explanation and never offered one. Sometimes, afterward, she would swing me in circles by my ankles, which thrilled me, or push me high on the swing. I loved her madly. When she took a job and only came home on weekends, I stood in the window and waited for hours for her Chevy to make the turn.

Neal has explained in advance that the service is usually divided into three sections. There are perhaps twenty people present, and the President, a local emergency room M.D., comments that in such a small congregation all available Mormons are drafted into frequent service. Consequently, during the service, he, his wife, his daughter, and his son all speak. The son kills two birds with one stone: participating in the Latter Day Saints service and earning a merit badge from the Boy Scouts in communication for delivering a speech longer than five minutes. Another of his daughters conducts us in the hymns. She seems to slide her fingers along the crests of imaginary waves, and our voices bob along in her wake.

Afterward, Neal and I go to my parents' and sit at the kitchen table for lunch. When he is in town, Neal always visits his grandparents after church. He sits alone with my father in the TV room and listens to his stories. This day, my father tells him an odd one: he says that his own father never talked to him when he was young, even when they worked side by side in the family bakery in Rochester. My grandfather, who was dead long before I got here, talked to everyone else, my father tells Neal, but never to him.

It is the first story I've ever heard in which my father expressed a lack of control, even vulnerability. My eyes fill with hot tears, and I peek into the TV room where he snoozes in his reclining chair, covered with an afghan even though it's hot as hell in the house. I wonder if he had anyone to talk to when he was young, like I had Shirley. He has her youngest son now, but it seems late, so late, too late.

Saturday

Yesterday, as I drove my mother to the grocery store, she mentioned that she was afraid last week, when she bent forward to put her daisies down on Shirley's casket, that she wasn't going to be able to stand up again. Too proud to sit in the car to wait, she had been on her feet for over an hour, waiting for the priest who forgot to come to her daughter's burial. She shifted from foot to foot in her beige stacked-heel pumps. It had been a bad week, a terrible week, for her: she seriously burned her finger and then slammed it in a drawer. It got infected. After everyone left her house, after the brunch that my sisters Joanie and Mary put together after Shirley's burial, my mother finally let her eldest daughter take her to the emergency room.

Every time Shirley's name is mentioned, my mother's eyes cloud over. Now, at the end of her life, she cries constantly. Actually, she always cried a lot, but now she cries mainly out of frustration because she has to "jump through knotholes," as she says, all day long for my demanding father, who runs her ragged from his recliner. "I'd like to knock him over a row of tin houses," she confides as she forces his oatmeal through a sieve before serving it to him. He complains, excessively, about lumps.

Yesterday, she summoned me to the living room where she showed me a cast iron trivet she had purchased but was keeping a big secret from her husband of seventy years. "The opinions expressed by the husband of this house are not necessarily those of the management," it says. Her eyes glitter when I read it, and she grasps my hand and giggles girlishly.

All week it has been cold, rainy, windy, buggy, miserable. On Wednesday, May 29th, it snowed all day. I sat with Marcia in her mountain cabin and watched the limbs of the spruce trees turn white. Snow collected on the heads of the hummingbirds at her bird feeder. At home, my lilac bushes were flattened, just a few purple flower tops peeking through a white lawn. I got onto my knees in the snow, lifted them up, and set them free.

The cold on my fingers carried me back to last November, to Shirley's kitchen, in which, every day, I bashed ice cubes into ice chips for her to suck on. I would get up early, cut cantaloupe into chunks, smash up a bag of ice chips, place a tumblerful of them by her bed, and give her her morning pills. Then I would exit so she could have her precious private time. I would come back hours later.

One morning, sleeping on the couch like I always did, I woke up to gorgeous organ music, church music, which seemed to be coming from upstairs. Oh, shit, I thought, not again, because thirty years ago, right after Shirley bought her house and moved in, I was sleeping on this same couch and I heard soft music from upstairs. I figured one of the kids had left a record player or a radio on, and I went upstairs to turn it off. I looked in each room. All six kids were sound asleep. I could still hear music, but I couldn't find the source. I woke Shirley up to tell her about it.

"You ought to lay off the pot," she whispered.

"I'm not high." I never smoked pot in her house, and she knew it.

She paused. "Maybe you were dreaming."

"I think I would know that," I said, faltering a little. Sometimes I get confused about where dreams end and reality begins.

She sat up in bed. "I don't hear anything," she said.

"Neither do I, now." In the end, we both shrugged. What else could we do?

I never heard music again, not in thirty years, until that night in November. I listened for several minutes, wondering if it was a figment of my imagination. Maybe I'm losing my mind, I thought.

Even though it was not even five o'clock in the morning and I knew Shirley desperately needed her sleep, I went into her bedroom and woke her up. "Shirley, do you hear music coming from upstairs?" Nobody but us had been in the house for several days, and I had not been upstairs since I last watered the plants up there. "I just want to know if you can hear it," I whispered.

A good sport, Shirley got up, which took time. I put a kitchen chair with her pillow on it at the bottom of the stairs, and she came shuffling out of the bedroom with her walker. She finally made it to the chair and sat down.

"Do you hear it?"

"Yes," she whispered, and we both peered up the dark staircase. It was an oddly breathless moment. "Go up and see what it is," she finally said.

"Who, me?"

"Yeah, you."

"You go," I stalled.

"Look, somebody's got to go, and I can't make it."

Of course, I knew that. "O.K.," I said, "O.K., I'll go."

I crept up a few stairs as ethereal organ music wafted around me. Then I stopped and looked over my shoulder. "Go," she said, "go." I can still see her intense brown eyes, urging me up, step by step.

It was just the radio. Jimmy told me later that he and Lisa had brought it over when they stayed one night, but I still don't know how it turned itself on or how it happened to be set on a church music station that I could never find again, nowhere on the dial.

Often, before she died, Shirley asked about the chimes, like church bells, that she heard far, far off in the distance. I never heard those. But sometimes, late at night or early in the morning, when it's very silent and my Shirley candle is lit, I think I hear that organ music again, and I find myself wondering if there's a radio playing upstairs in my sister's empty house.

Kingdom Hall of the Jehovah's Witnesses
Malone, NY

After two weeks in the North Country I am sleepwalking, which always happens to me here and I don't know exactly why, though it has everything to do with my parents. Without meaning to, without trying to, without noticing that they have done it, they unwrap me. My fifty years are nothing more than swaddling clothes, easily removed to leave me exposed and helpless. My personality disappears. I sit in a chair in their TV room like a lump and nod my head yes even when I disagree. I find this enormously depressing. So is the rain. It has rained or snowed every day since I've been here. The snowfall of a few days ago not only forced the lilacs to the ground but also snapped the necks of Robert's pretty lupins. I have doubled my daily dose of St. John's Wort as a way of fighting back.

I am parked outside the Kingdom Hall of the Jehovah's Witnesses listening to an interview with the great blues man, Robert Cray. The announcer asks him what we, the regular people, would know if we had

had his life and experience instead of our own. Robert Cray says, "How open people are to the blues, all over the world."

I don't feel open to the blues today, but they have found me anyway. Through the rain, I watch cars pull up under the portal in front of the church, where the drivers, the men, let out the women and little children. I wish I were far away from the North Country, back in New Mexico where the sun shines every day. I am shocked by my reflection in the window. I am old. I lean forward to study the maroon bags under my eyes.

I have just spent the night at my parents' house. All night long, my father hacked and coughed. I could hear the crap in his chest rattle and crackle from the living room, where I slept on the couch. His lungs want to shut down, and every breath is like a crack of lightning into them. He gets disoriented in the night and doesn't know what he's doing. The two helpers my mother has hired to spend five nights a week say he often talks to his own father in the night. He calls him Pop. After all these years, my father is still trying to talk to Pop, and Pop is still not answering.

Or maybe, at last, he is.

I hate my nights on father duty: the blasting television, my parents' bickering, the death rattle in my father's chest. I am ashamed to say that I resent everything I have to do for him. For Shirley, I tried to provide comfort in every moment, and I did it with deep pleasure most of the time. I did it with love. At my father's, I count the hours until Saturday night is over and I can legitimately take off for Sunday church.

Like a list-making minister, I try to sort out my turbulent emotions, categorize and make sense of them. I understand love, even if it is complicated in its variety of forms and its unpredictable ebb and flow. It lifts you up and carries you, and even if you don't know where you're going, you are not afraid. But I can't figure out the sense of duty that compelled me to return to my father's sickbed. I feel so little that's specifically connected to him. I have general compassion, the deep sadness with which we observe the old and helpless. But I can't feel anything for him personally.

When I was a little girl in braids, I was certain that my father loved me, but that abruptly ended somewhere before puberty. After that, he seemed to dislike me. That dislike escalated, and within a few short years, he detested me. And, I admit, the feeling became mutual. So why am I here?

Even as my father and I have inched our way toward each other, tolerance has increased but not love. Sitting in these Christian churches, with Adams and Eves in the stained glass windows, I sometimes wonder if Paradise, the Garden of Eden, is nothing more than the state of feeling loved. I got booted out of the Garden, and here I am, forty years later, looking for a way back in. But, believe me, there is no door.

According to my self-created grief management plan, I am supposed to meditate this week on my hippie years. Those were the years my father hated me the most. The year he threw me out of the house, out of the family. I can't forget the names he called me. The ways he tried to break my spirit. And the many years we refused to speak. Once Shirley orchestrated a visit between me and my parents, whom I had not seen in about three years. My father was standing in the driveway when we pulled in. I got out of the car. He looked at me with disgust. "You're fat," he hissed. Those were the only words exchanged during the reunion. Even Shirley was speechless.

But those were also the years when I came to Shirley's and stayed for months. She welcomed me every time, and my friends, too. Her door, her pocketbook, and her heart were wide open to me, and whatever hope I had in life and whatever love I experienced was rooted in my visits to Dow Road. There was freedom for me through Shirley. There was joy and connection and a place to come home to, a place to belong. It was beautiful for me. It really was.

Remembering it, I feel warm as I run through the rain to the door. When I step over the threshold, I immediately run into Linda, a Witness who long ago used to visit Shirley. They spent many afternoons at the kitchen table discussing Biblical fine points. Linda continued to stop by forever after. She offered many times to relieve me, to stay with Shirley as a nurse, but I never asked her to. "How's your father?" she asks.

"Bad."

Linda nods. There is really nothing to say.

I move to a seat in the middle of a large, plain room. There are no images at all, and just one framed inspirational message: "Stand complete with firm conviction in all the will of God." The Kingdom Hall fills up—seventy-four people, they announce—but we don't do very well with the first hymn. We stagger, musically, through four verses and then give up. An opening prayer of thanks is said, and then Brother Hill, a visiting speaker from a town twenty-five miles away, is introduced. His sermon, "Come You that Thirst for the Truth," begins with a severe warning about making spiritual errors, specifically, the error of believing in an eternal soul. The Bible is clear on this, Brother Hill says. I jot down his words: "There is no continuous consciousness in the death state."

Yet this past week my sister Laurie's husband, John (whom I call "the Murph") was driving home after a long day at his two jobs. His car was threatening to crap out—an event which happens to the Murph with alarming regularity. He barely made it home, and early the next morning he coaxed the car into the repair shop—"Where Poochie's Rags to Riches used to be," he said—but the mechanic wasn't there yet, so the Murph bucked on to the real estate office where he works, part-time. His mood darkened even more, and he couldn't concentrate, so he decided to drive back to the garage. As he putted down Route 11, he saw a woman walking toward him in the rain, along the edge of the highway. She wore a heavy winter coat. As he drove by, the Murph glanced over at her, and she smiled.

It was Shirley.

A feeling of total euphoria and intense wellbeing flooded over John. Suddenly, he said, everything was perfect. He drove into the garage, where the mechanic was standing outside as if he'd been waiting for John to show up. This mechanic reached into his pocket, took out a part, installed it on the car in two minutes, refused to charge him a penny, and sent John on his merry way.

John, whom Shirley loved, was the "Master of Ceremonies" at Shirley's memorial service. Near its end, he said he felt compelled to add something personal. He began by identifying himself as a sports lover and then said that he, while watching sports on satellite TV, often asks his sons a rhetorical question: What makes a great player? The answer, said John, is this: a great player makes his teammates *better*. John said that was what Shirley did. She made us all better.

Brother Hill, and probably the rest of the Witnesses, would laugh, or worse, at John, I guess. According to them, Shirley is six feet under, waiting for the resurrection. I don't know where she is, but I don't think she's six feet under. I have driven by the cemetery twice, pulled to the side of the road, and stared out over the field of graves. Even the flowers are gone from Shirley's now. I don't believe she's there.

Like Pastor Roberts from the First Christian Church two weeks ago,

Brother Hill is into lists. There are three ways to find the truth, he says:

1) cultivate a thirst for it by becoming conscious of your own religious needs;
2) formulate a reasonable and consistent set of values;
3) reject religious error, such as the concept of the immortal soul.

He has four suggestions on how to develop spiritual thirst, but I allow my mind to wander. Here in the North Country, I often wander, aimless and confused. Once a week I come to church, my main landmark, and that is all I know. Sometimes I don't learn anything in church, but sometimes I do. For example, today we study an article in the *Watchtower* which states that there are 45,000 thunder and lightning storms a day on Planet Earth, 1.6 million a year, 2000 are happening somewhere right now, and the energy in each is as powerful as ten nuclear bombs.

At the end, as we mill toward the door, a few women introduce themselves and ask me where I'm from. "New Mexico," I say, although Robert and I own a house right here, free and clear, and my roots go several generations into this earth.

"Are you a member of a congregation there?" one elderly lady asks.

"I'm not a member of any church at all," I announce. "I'm just doing research."

"Research? Oh my," she responds. I think about this as I drive home. In order to develop spiritual thirst, Brother Hill said today, one has to develop consciousness of a spiritual need. I have had both the consciousness and the need for my whole life, but it got unceremoniously extinguished when I watched my sister slowly die. Now I attend church, hoping for a resurrection, but, like a corpse, I am no longer thirsty. It makes me angry and defiant. It's all gone, all gone, I want to shout.

Today, this, and the rain, give me the blues.

Wednesday

Last night, I had this dream:

When it was time to remove Shirley's body from the vault to bury her, we discovered that she was not dead. She was weak, very weak, but alive. Resurrected. She seemed extraordinarily calm, and her skin looked dewy. I felt tremendous peace in the room and I wanted to ask her about this miracle—her resurrection—but I could not collect the words.

I woke up remembering the old Shirley, the young Shirley, the other Shirley. I hadn't noticed how accustomed I had become to the later Shirley, the dying Shirley, the exhausted, emaciated, dehydrated Shirley. I lay in bed luxuriating in this different version of my sister. Shirley circa 1984. The Shirley of Jack's picture.

Yesterday, I asked my parents what they thought of the Murph's vision. "I believe it completely," my mother said, immediately and with conviction. Long before Shirley was officially diagnosed, when all that had happened was that she suddenly despised coffee, my mother had woken up from a terrible dream. "There was a little girl with pigtails standing by the side of my bed," my mother reported in a shaky voice. "It was Shirley." It was a bad omen, she said. My mother's superstitious nature fascinates me. She will eat standing up in the kitchen rather than set thirteen places at the table. She goes pale if a bird flies into the house. During my hippie years, she placed a photo of me on her dresser mirror overlapping one of her dead father as a way to secure his protection.

I find it odd that the Jehovah's Witnesses' sermon of Sunday attacked the notion of continued consciousness after death while the Murph's vision relies on it.

I turn to my father. "What do you think?"

"These things happen," he says. "I have documented proof."

"Really?" This I find interesting. Usually I can—everyone can—recite his stories right along with him. Most have a climax in which he grabs somebody by the neck and says, "Brother, you're about to learn a lesson." My father grew up scrapping in neighborhoods crowded with tough, white European immigrants. As a boy, he once broke his arm but didn't tell his parents because they had another son, Joey, who was dying of blood poisoning. My father sucked it up—the pain of a broken arm—until his ten-year-old brother's funeral was over. He collected mercury out of broken thermometers behind a factory in his neighborhood, by hand, and sold it to bring in grocery money. Later, he boxed in carnivals and circuses and wrestled for prize money. He augmented his measly phys ed teacher's salary by being the guy nobody could knock out in the boxing ring during the Depression. And during Vietnam, my father often said that "they" should send him over there as a secret weapon. "Yeah? What would *you* do?" I asked, sullenly. "I'd settle it with these!" he would answer, raising his two fists in front of him and staring at me murderously. Now he can barely move. He cannot stand up. His big adventure everyday is a short walk into the bathroom, where he shaves. He weighs 105 pounds.

"Three times I had dreams and they came true," my father explains. "Mother can corroborate this. I told her my dreams, and then they happened." My mother is nodding from her matching reclining chair.

"What were they?" I am not pretending to be interested.

"The first one was about my brother, Art. In my dream, I saw him wading with a bunch of other guys in water. And then I saw his arms go up like this." He demonstrates, lifting his skinny arms high above his head in a spastic jerk. "This was during World War II." His brother was killed the day he had the dream. Maybe the minute.

The second dream was about Dave Smurl. This was Art's wife Rosie's second husband. One night in the mid-sixties, my father had a dream that Dave was calling out to him for help. "He was in the backyard at West Point, I thought," my father said, "going round and round in circles. Round and round. I tried to get to him, but I couldn't." My father woke up and told this to my mother. The next day, Rosie called. Dave had died of a heart attack alone in his boat while fishing on the Long Island Sound. When he was found, by strangers, the boat, with no one left to steer it, was circling round and round.

In the third dream, my mother's sister's husband, Eddy (a great friend of my father's), was at work at the Reynold's aluminum plant. In the dream, a machine blew up, and Eddy was seriously burned. In the morning, my parents learned that there had been an accident. Eddy was working nights. A machine blew at the plant. He was in bad shape.

I feel a lightening inside my ribcage, as if there's suddenly more breathing room. My father's dreams, added to John's vision, make me believe that Shirley, or some form of her, was really, truly walking down the side of the road the other day when the Murph sputtered by in his old Escort.

"Do you ever have any dreams about Shirley?" I ask my father.

"No. Never."

I think, have thought for months, that whereas Shirley was very brave, my father is afraid to die. Lately, he insists that my mother stay in the TV room with him, all the time. If he's left alone, even for a few minutes, he hollers for her. He is driving her crazy.

I am waiting up when Robert gets home from work, and I tell him what my father said. "Why does my father get to get these dreams?" I demand. "He's about as sensitive as a Mack truck."

"Maybe he needs them more than anybody else," Robert replies.

"Damn it, I want dreams like that. I want dream proof," I say. "I'm the one who's on a quest here. I'm the one who's going to a different friggin' church every week."

"Maybe that's why you don't need the dreams."

I do not respond.

In the morning darkness, my Shirley candle burns. I cannot think about continued consciousness after death or why my father saw Dave Smurl circling around the back yard. Today, all I can do is make a future plan: when my *Month of Sundays* is over, I will express mail my Shirley candle to my nephew Jimmy. I will ask him to bury it for me in Shirley's garden. It will be our secret.

First Congregational Church
Malone, NY

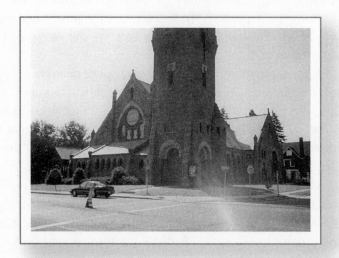

I parallel park down the block from the First Congregational Church. It is a gorgeous stone building with a slate roof and a Gothic tower that, according to the Murph, was used for reconnaissance when Malone was a stop on the Underground Railroad. The Murph says there are tunnels all under the town, accessible through the basement of this church. I am patiently waiting for church long before the bell begins to toll. I don't have to ask for whom it tolls.

I enter by a side door, choose a pew, and sit down. Several people stare down on the congregation from the choir loft, which stretches across the front of the church at a height of about fifteen feet. It's like facing a tribunal in seventeenth century England. In fact, this whole church has an English feeling. On the wall directly in front of me is a brass plaque:

Ashbel Parmelee, D.D.
Born October 18, 1784

instantly translated
into the heavenly kingdom
May 24, 1862

Instantly translated to the heavenly kingdom? This sounds good, though I can't imagine who would have the confidence to say it, think it, or carve it onto a plaque. My sister was very slowly and painfully translated, and if the Murph's vision is correct, she may not be fully translated even now.

It strikes me quite funny, though, the concept of death being reduced to a mere translation. Life is one language, death is another, and the translation, if it's accurate, keeps the meaning intact. I lean back into the pew and suppress a giggle. Ever since it became clear that Shirley was going to die, I've been either obsessed with discovering the meaning or terrified that there isn't any. I have had the idea that facing this mystery, living in and with it, is a worthwhile quest, even a noble one.

But suddenly I realize that launching a relentless search for meaning is a damn good way to miss out on the here and now. I once read, in a government pamphlet written for distribution to foreign professionals working in the USA, that Americans typically ignore the past, live in and for the future, and are oblivious to the present. Oblivious, it said.

I sit up straight, determined to be where I am, and the service begins. Hymns are energetically performed by the choir, and then we are greeted by the pastor, the Reverend Mr. John Werley, who wears a white robe, a white rope belt, and a red stole. Together, we recite the introductory prayer printed in the bulletin:

> People of God, look about; see the faces of those we know
> and love
> Neighbors and friends, sisters and brothers—a community
> of kindred spirits.
> People of God, look about and see the faces of those we
> hardly know—
> Strangers, sojourners, forgotten friends, the ones who need
> an outstretched hand.
> People of God, look about and see all the images of God
> assembled here.
> In me, in you, in each of us, God's spirit shines for all to see.

> People of God, come. Let us confess our sins together as we
> enter into the presence of the Triune God.

The Reverend Mr. Werley preaches on "Unity in Diversity." He sounds downright mad as he describes problems he has with the authoritarian policymakers of his own church, but then he segues into the message that all believers in Christ are unified in and by their belief. Of course, there will be diversity of personality and opinion, just like there is within his church, but the overarching unity is the belief in Jesus Christ as savior. God is diverse, he says, and the trinity is a symbol: God the Father is the creator; God the Son is the redeemer; and God the Holy Spirit sanctifies. Three in one.

How many people am I?

One of me, at least, is reckless, pairing in my mind my sister's recent death and my father's imminent one, remembering them together as if they are joined at the hip. I am on a collision course: my sister and father colliding, the past and the present smashing up against each other. But I see in bright detail how Shirley soothed the pain out of me, how she neutralized my hurt, how she stood like a pillar of love that nobody, and I mean nobody, could topple. Without Shirley, I would have been a goner.

Instantly translated into nothingness.

Nothing but darkness without Shirley.

Wednesday

A few months after Robert and I got married, twelve years ago, we bought a rundown farm house on the side of the northernmost peak in the Adirondack mountain chain, just seven miles from my parents. It seemed like a good idea at the time. My sister Laurie picked it out, and we bought it sight unseen because it was dirt cheap. We were living in Los Angeles, where similar houses cost two-hundred-thousand bucks.

Part of the reason, part of my reason, for buying it was to be close enough to my father to reconcile with him before he died. I don't think I admitted that to myself at the time, or maybe I didn't even know it. When we arrived for the first summer, I tiptoed around and kept my mouth shut in my father's presence, and he did likewise. We established an armed truce, broken only periodically, like the time I told him I'd had a dream in which the novel I was writing was lost somewhere in his house, and he replied, in real life, "Well, I ran out of toilet paper, so I used it to wipe my rear." There were a few low points like that, but overall it was a little better between us.

Shirley, who lived a half hour away, came to our little house several times a week. She painted, wall papered, and stripped cabinets, floors, and wainscoting. She dragged off the crappy old furniture that came with the house and returned glorious antiques. I did five percent of the work and talked one-hundred times as much as Shirley. Every day, when she put on her nurse's aide uniform and went to work for the evening shift, I felt a little stab of loneliness. The next day, I would find myself waiting at the window, watching for her car to turn in the driveway, just as I did when I was a child and she was working at the *Reader's Digest*. I had not been around the North Country much for years, maybe fifteen, and being with Shirley was precious. What was drained out of me daily by toning myself down around my father was replenished by the presence of my sister. She made me feel vibrant with color, whereas my father left me feeling anemic and pasty-faced. Shirley saw beauty in everything. She lived in it. My father griped non-stop, as if he fervently believed he was making a contribution to the world with his criticism. It was exhausting to be around him and hard to shake off the negativity he generated.

One day, when I was complaining about this to Shirley, it hit me that I was acting just like him. Bitching and moaning. I vowed to try to keep the lid on it, especially around Shirley, who didn't need to be subjected by proxy to my father's negativity. It wasn't easy.

By the end of the summer, when Robert and I returned to Los Angeles, I was re-glued to my sister. Then, the next summer, the year I turned forty and gave up on a career as a screenwriter, we moved there, and the blank period began.

The day after we arrived, I sped to Shirley's house. I felt giddy barreling down Dow Road, under the canopy of huge old hardwood trees. I found her in her kitchen. The TV was tuned to a soap opera.

"I have returned!" I announced from the doorway, like a victorious army general. "Resident of the North Country!"

"I hope you know what you're doing," she said. Her tone sounded sinister. This was before she even stood up, before she turned the TV down, but not off. All the while we talked, her eyes drifted to its screen and caught there. Clearly, I was playing second fiddle to the boob tube. Somehow, I hid my anger from Shirley, but driving home, I let her have it. "Great to see you, too," I spat, cynically, into the humid air. "Don't let ME interrupt you."

The side jokes between us at the Sunday dinner table petered out. She didn't come up to work on my house anymore. Her closest friend was killed in a car accident, and she didn't even call me. When I showed up in her kitchen to grieve with her, she left me sitting there and disappeared into her bedroom. After a while, I just left.

Shirley didn't seem to love me anymore, and I went into a tailspin.

And the numbness set in.

Such a catastrophic break, the end of the family love era in my personal life, deserved more than numbness, distance, and a poisonous concoction of regret and resentment that continuously simmered in my heart, just below the boiling point. I felt this strongly at the time, but I was helpless to change it. If there had only been vicious words, some precious object broken in rage, a brawl, I could have handled it. With such things, there is always a road back, paved with tears and apologies and promises never to slip so far again. But none of that happened between me and my sister.

Instead, we seemed to have moved into a vacuum with nothing but dead air between us. There was suddenly nothing to say, no feeling of connection, nothing. The Shirley I knew and counted on had disappeared, leaving me adrift in the emotions she had always soothed by her simple, powerful presence.

I tried to be adult about it. I began to seriously edit myself in conversation in an attempt to isolate and remove whatever was driving her from me. I told myself I was too old to be so needy and dependent, and that Shirley had entered a different part of life, out of the mother role and into the crone phase, and she needed privacy to adjust to it. Sitting up late with Mr. Boston cognac for company, I agonized and analyzed and mentally replayed each of our visits together, searching for clues.

I came up with nothing.

Except that it was meaningless, our relationship.

And, being me, prone to feel fated to the worst case scenario, I extrapolated that backwards. I told myself it probably always had been meaningless, that I had fooled myself all along, that this was the way Shirley had always felt about me, though she hadn't had the courage to show it until now. The illusion was over. My borrowed time was up. It was back to reality. No hope.

I felt debilitated by my inner turbulence. Once, during this time, I ran into Shirley's friend Marcia in the post office, and she started to say something about Shirley, and I held my hand up in a stop gesture and hurried past her to my car. I cried a lot. But I never went to Shirley to talk about it, not once in the whole year we lived there. I felt banished from her presence. Exiled against my will. And after that, as the years rolled by and the distance hardened, I think I blamed her for yanking the rug out from under me.

But lately, sitting on my porch swing when it's very dark and cool, I think about it a different way. I remember packing up and leaving L.A., running home to Shirley with great expectations. Expecting everything, really. There wasn't any way it could go but down, given the hugeness of my need for her perfection and her unconditional love. I'm actually amazed that she lasted, or anyone could last, forty years on the pedestal.

My friend Julie Shigekuni recently told me that she finds the way I operate in life to be very puzzling. "You have a perception, and you mull it over and mull it over until it becomes reality, and then you go on from there," she said. Factoring this into my memories of the blank years, I wonder if perhaps I took a small rejection, or a series of them, or a moment of awkwardness and disconnect, and built it into the wall between us. I wonder if I created my own exile. If I imagined it worse than it was and just went on from there.

Besides, the red rage I felt inside of me the soap opera day in Shirley's kitchen—that was not my first experience of it. It is a force that possesses and consumes me when I feel vulnerable and have an intense need for something, usually small, that I don't get. Rejection, no matter how insignificant if the circumstances are just right, triggers it, and when it takes me over, I am on the warpath, and bloodthirsty. Once, back in New Mexico, I needed to arrange a ride home from the hospital after having had a small surgery on my bottom lip. I asked Julie Reichert if she could pick me up, and she hesitated for about two seconds, probably reviewing her day's calendar in her mind, but before she could answer, I went ballistic. "Forget it!" I snapped, throwing an unconscious karate chop in her direction before I stormed out, fuming, convinced I needed to cut her out of my life completely.

This blind rage that overtakes me when I feel temporarily dependent is terrifying to me. I am capable of serious destruction when I'm in its grip. But in the safety of my porch swing, late at night, it has begun to seem like a key capable of opening some simple truth. I connect the rage with my father because it is so like his. And because I'm pretty sure that his rejection of me when I needed his acceptance so desperately is what created it in the first place. This irrational rage is like a physical place that I get delivered to where my own survival is the central, or only, issue. There is usually relationship devastation in its wake. Or, as an alternative, numbness.

On the porch swing, I close my eyes and in those hypnagogic images that appear like a miracle inside the eyelids, I see Shirley and me in a kind of dance. We are not far apart, but the movement of the dance seems to be backwards, away from each other. We retreat in synch, mimicking each other's every move. Then I realize what I am seeing is a mirror with my sister on one side and me on the other. Even if we come to the front, to the surface, which we don't, we would be separated, locked on our own side of the glass.

Somehow, oddly, I find this dancing-away image comforting. There were two of us there in the blank years, after all. Neither one of us hollered, "Hey! What's this all about?" We just danced away, farther and farther, until even the memory of closeness began to fade. I will never know what Shirley thought at that time, but I imagine she was a little afraid of me. She had never seen that side, after all, the side that retreats and then grows cold.

She was probably as baffled and as hurt as I was.

Temple Shalom
Salem, MA

I am sitting on my niece Julie's deck at seven in the morning, and the sun is blazing through the moisture in the air. When I came out here, the little patch of harbor visible through the rooftops was grey-blue. So many sailboats were moored there that their masts looked like a forest of skinny trees. Less than an hour later, the sun blasts like a spotlight behind a scrim, and everything has turned white. I have to squint and then go inside for sunglasses. This is my only Sunday here in Salem, Massachusetts, where I have spent the past few days. I am worried about Julie, whose first thought every morning is, I'm a total wreck.

Being in Salem, I hope for a Sunday Wicca service, some witchiness or at least an earth-based worship that incorporates the sun, moon, stars, and earth, but I find nothing, not even in the special "Witchcraft" section of the Yellow Pages. I opt for a Jewish synagogue, the Temple Shalom, where there is a service at eight in the morning on Sunday. But at ten of, there is no activity, and I begin to suspect that G-d is going to stand me up again. I circle around to the side, where an elderly woman and man stand.

"Is there a service today?" I ask.

"If we get a minyan," the woman, Roz, answers.

"Excuse me, I'm not Jewish."

"Ten people." We all look around. A tall man wearing a spandex bicycle outfit chats with three other cyclists on the sidewalk. "Are they here for the service?" I ask.

"Just the tall, grey-haired guy."

"So we got four," I observe.

"You don't count," the woman says.

A laugh erupts like a yelp from my throat. It is refreshing to be dismissed so efficiently, one clean swipe of the sword. In a way, though, it's not fair. I should count because I am doing my assignment. I just didn't know how big it was. The story of my grief is a web, just as Leslie Marmon Silko described, with Shirley at the center. But the lines that crisscross over each other as the more complex story unfolds surprise me. I am caught in a maze of images and ideas—everything from faith and God to life and death, from charismatics to medicine men, from the rapture to purgatory and onward to hell. And time is not accurate in this altered space either. My past, present, and future have collapsed in on one another. I go from five years old to fifty and back again in the blink of an eye. My family connections, the stickiest part of the story, weave it all together, and there is no escape. My father, my sister, and I are trapped in this story, and there is no point in denying it.

Of course, I do not mention any of this to my two companions. A car pulls up and three very senior citizens struggle out. "The average age of the members of this congregation is eighty," Roz whispers, "but they're in their nineties." As they shuffle across the street, three of the cyclists peddle away, and the fourth, who turns out to be the ex-mayor of Salem, joins us. "Let's do it," he says decisively as he chains his bike up to the railing. "Let's do it."

I am introduced as a visitor, and the ex-mayor, who wears a helmet and goggles as he talks, lectures me for a few minutes: "The Jewish community was established in Salem pre Civil War," he begins. "Most Jewish communities in the east were established in the 1880s after the wave of European immigration, but we were already here. At one point, we had 4,000 Jews in a population of about 40,000." But now, there is not even a minyan. On our way inside, Roz explains that they have not had a rabbi here for eight or nine years. "We hired one to start in July," she says, raising her eyebrows gleefully. "A woman."

The chapel is tiny and plain. Before I can even glance around, the men have put on their prayer shawls and yarmulkes, and one of them has gone to the front and opened the Torah. Roz hands me a book, which I open backwards, upside down, every which way until I get it right and start from the back. Hebrew is on the right and English is on the left.

In front, one man calls out Hebrew prayers, while the ex-mayor walks up and down, up and down the center aisle, singing responses. When I studied at the temple of tarot in L.A., I was required to learn the Hebrew alphabet because a Hebrew letter is assigned to each of the keys in the Major Arcana, and the foundation of tarot meditation is in Kabala. I am actually able to recite one of the prayers in Hebrew because we sang it every Sunday in the tarot temple. I glance at the English translation, remembering: Hear, Oh Israel, the Lord is one.

Pages turn, men bow, and strong male voices chant. I haven't the foggiest idea what's going on, and it doesn't matter one bit. I don't know where I am in the web today, and there is simply no use in pretending I do.

Friday

I wake up from another burial dream. This burial is New Orleans style, with a parade of musicians. A young black woman with red-tipped dreadlocks is featured. She plays a wind instrument, maybe a flute or clarinet. I am not sure when I wake whose burial it is, but I am saying, "All things come to an end, and, oh, what an end it was."

In the tradition of Jungian dream interpretation, I imagine myself as both characters in the dream: the black woman making music and the dead body, too. If a part of me could be buried once and for all, I have no doubt which aspect of myself I would offer up—the part that's caught in the web of the past, trapped in old pain that does me no good whatsoever.

I keep going over it in my mind—how, as my relationship with my father creaked open, minimally, the deep intimacy with Shirley closed down. I replay it again and again, how Robert and I, consumed with the notion of starting over as less ambitious (and frustrated) people, moved from L.A. to our little farmhouse in the North Country. We got jobs, but nothing went right, and soon we blasted through our savings just attempting to make the house livable, with water and heat. Winter came, with its forty-below-zero nights. Inside, we froze. I started to drink Mr. Boston cognac.

Being around my parents put me in a deep black hole. There was surface reconciliation but no deep connection. I started to drive carelessly over the icy roads, ending up in a ditch again and again. Almost every night, I would skid the truck against the maple tree as I tried to back into the driveway. Robert, cursing, would dig it out. I started to itch so terribly that I'd scratch my arms, legs, and back raw and bleeding, and keep right on scratching.

We ran out of money. I had, on the last business hour of the last business day I was in L.A., after we had let our apartment go and packed the truck for the move, snagged a small screenwriting job, and I could not produce the work. It snowed every single day, and there was no color anywhere. White sky, white snow, white world. Once, the temperature went up to zero, and I insisted that Robert take a walk with me. We began to bicker, like my parents. "You're just like your father," he often said, his greatest insult.

All through this, hands-down the worst year of my life, I almost never saw Shirley, except at the mandatory, paralyzing Sunday dinners. I made excuses for her: her last kid had finally grown up and gone, and she needed the peace and private time she had craved for three decades. Her blood pressure was high, and she didn't feel good. I was a stone drag, and she was sick of me and my histrionics, my depression, my dramatic disappointment. Maybe she'd just had enough of taking care of people. After all, she was an aide in a nursing home, wiping asses for minimum wage. And I was forty, a grownup, and shouldn't be depending on her anyway.

But that didn't matter to me. To me, the blank space, Shirley missing from my life, was all I could see or feel. If Shirley, the embodiment of unconditional love, could turn away, turn off, and disappear, then what was the point? When my father turned against me, decades before, I withdrew emotionally and then, as soon as I could, I ran away. And when Shirley disappeared, I hustled up a job in New York City, four-hundred miles away, and moved there. Robert stayed behind. We needed distance, a lot of it. Before I left, I called Shirley. "If you ever want to talk about what happened here this year, let me know," I said.

"How about now?" she responded.

I took a deep breath, "Well Shirley, you've been totally unavailable," I said. "Just gone. You make it clear that you don't want anybody around, including me. You don't even talk to me."

"What can I talk about?" my sister said. "You're so much more educated than me."

I was floored.

"Besides," she added, "you're married now."

None of it made sense.

"That is such a crock of shit," I said. "I have been desperate to see you. Desperate. And now I'm leaving, and it's all too late." All I can say, looking back, is that it felt too late. It did.

We hung up, and the numbness started. There was no hatred, no rage, no more accusations. Just the big blank, the chasm into which the next years fell. I didn't blame Shirley. I blamed myself. I had failed her. Something was wrong with her, something had happened, and I should have gone in like a bulldozer, dug until I uncovered the problem, and then healed it.

But I didn't. I did nothing but take off. I let her be, to sink or swim on her own.

Nearly ten years drifted by. She got sick. I made that phone call. "I'm one of the people who cares about you," I said, the words sticking in my throat.

Don't admit you care. Don't show it. Don't love. Don't trust. Don't open yourself up for the pain of being shut out, rejected, or, worse, helpless. I look to my father, my eyes murderous this time. My inheritance.

I remember one time in the hippie years, when I visited Shirley. I was obsessed with "I Stand Here Ironing" by Tillie Olson. I asked Shirley to read it to me, and it's long, because I needed to hear it read in a mother's voice. It is the story of a mother, thinking about her daughter, and it ends, "Only help her to know—help make it so there is cause for her to know—that she is more than this dress on the ironing board, helpless before the iron." That has been how I felt, helpless before the iron my whole life, with nobody but Shirley to know or care. And now she was helpless before the iron, too.

So I went back. I bulldozed in on my spring break, making her talk to me. "On a scale of one to ten, how much pain? Name your symptoms. Talk to me about getting up in the night, taking baths for relief. How many times did you shit in the last three months?" (The answer, once, terrified me.) I ordered the blood test for cancer markers in the pancreatic enzymes. It came back positive. Back in New Mexico, when I heard this, I ran back to Shirley. I ran back for my life.

Suddenly, a father-memory intrudes. A good one. On Sundays, after church, my father would take my little sister, Laurie, and me to the gym where he worked for twenty-nine years. It was closed to cadets until noon. He would sit in his office cubicle, and we would swim in the Olympic-sized pool. With no supervision, we would jump off the balcony into the chlorinated green water. We did endless repetitions of Venus rising from the sea. We did cannonballs from the diving boards.

On the wall of the pool room was a large West Point-style sign: When the going gets tough, the tough get going. Suddenly, I realize that I, like generations of cadets, got going all right. When the going got tough, I got going. Away. Inside. Gone. But in the end, in the nick of time, I learned a lesson. Love is something you have to give in order to get. And the readiness is all.

I stare out the window at the workshop Robert is building. The wood has a yellow glow against the blue sky, but soon it will turn grey, like the rest of the barns in the North Country. Like Shirley's barns. One by one, her out buildings have collapsed: the milk house, the tool shed, the big barn. There is only one left standing now, and it is listing heavily to the right. Jimmy has jacked it up, but every year it leans a little more. Shirley could not afford to maintain these buildings. She could hardly keep the house going while the kids were growing up.

It's strange about things falling down, returning to the earth. Burial is strange. I have never liked it as a concept: the rotting in a box, six feet underground; the receding features, the emerging skeleton, the postmortem growth of the hair and fingernails. But having buried Shirley, all that suddenly seems fine and natural. Just like her dying did, once I accepted it as inevitable. In Stage Two of the Final Dive, Shirley asked me, "Why can't you just let it be what it is?"

Maybe I am, Shirley, I think. Maybe I am.

Church of the Assumption
Gabriels, NY

Yesterday, on a pilgrimage to the health food store in Saranac Lake, I passed through the town of Gabriels, where I noticed the Church of the Assumption on the right and made a snap decision to go there today. I have spent the night on father duty. My father faces his final days with a red hot mixture of anger at his incapacity, frustration with his helplessness, and restless agitation. He remains alert for twenty or more hours a day. At ninety-four, he can't even get a good night's sleep because he goes "squirrelly," as my sister Janet puts it, on even a mild dose of sleeping pills. He cannot stop thinking. His brain just keeps on grinding. "The mind is a terrible thing to keep," I say to my friend Michele, who sometimes worries that her own aging mother is losing hers. When I stay at my parents' on the weekends, I often develop a dread that it is my destiny, too, to live, wide awake, into my nineties, with my mind on full steam ahead.

Shirley, on the other hand, surrendered gracefully. Her body lasted as long as it could, and her mind stayed remarkably steady. And when she took the Final Dive, she went inward (losing consciousness) and away at the same time. The whole year-long event was choreographed with exceptional elegance, which is what her best friend Marcia spoke about at Shirley's memorial service.

Marcia said:

> It is an honor to have Shirley call me her friend and to say a few words about Shirley. The word that always comes to my mind about Shirley is "elegant." Elegant: refined grace, restrained beauty, dignified propriety.
>
> It takes great courage to be truly elegant, and Shirley Carter was an elegant woman. She was elegant as a nurse's aide, where I first met her, caring with dignity, and certainly elegant as my friend, which was not always an easy task. She was elegant as a daughter and sister. And most elegant as a mother, as is evidenced by the legacy of her children here. We know the meaning of elegance because of Shirley. That is what she gave us, and we are blessed to have had her in our lives
>
> I thought of telling "stories" of Shirley, but this poem found its way to me and it says it all, far better than I could:
>
> One night
> there's a heartbeat at the door
> Outside, a woman in the fog,
> with hair of twigs and dress of weed
> dripping green lake water.
> She says,
> "I am you, and I have
> traveled a long distance.
> Come with me; there is something
> I must show you"—
> She turns to go, her cloak falls open
> Suddenly,

Golden light—everywhere
Golden light.

Shirley is our golden light, shining her love over us all.

The light today is golden, too, and Shirley would have loved it. I am gunning her car to church, doing seventy-five m.p.h. along Route 30 because I am late for church and it is a long drive.

This morning, while I was having coffee, my mother suggested I attend only Roman Catholic churches for my whole *Month*. "Get the real thing," she advised.

"Don't get your hopes up, Ma," I responded, testily. "I'm not going to become a Catholic, like Shirley did." I was livid, enraged, blinded by anger last summer when my mother sent that nun and priest to pressure Shirley back into the church. She had no intention then, pre-Paul, of returning to the religion that had let her down. In a letter, much later, Mary said:

> Shirley's dissatisfaction with Catholicism came about through the abuses of the clergy and the Vatican as much as anything else. She saw the selling of annulments in much the same way as Martin Luther had seen the selling of indulgences. She thought there was corruption in the church and she didn't condone it. Shirley told me that she felt like a hypocrite going to church and that the church itself was filled with hypocrites and she didn't want to be among them. But she missed it. I think that's when she began relying more on reading the Bible.

That day last summer, I snapped at my mother, "Why don't you leave Shirley alone? She's got enough on her mind without you sending in the Catholic cavalry."

"I want her to have the last rites," my mother replied, so adamant about it that she didn't even raise her voice. In the end, she got what she wanted, and I hope, and I have to believe, that Shirley did, too.

The service at the Church of the Assumption is very short, a tradition in the summer in the North Country, when people want to be outside in the precious sun. Stand up, sit down, kneel. Stand up, sit down, beat heart, sing. This church is painted sky blue above the wainscoting, and the corners and edges of the ceiling are rounded, creating a sense of endless azure sky-space.

In his sermon, the priest quotes Mother Teresa. I actually own a documentary of the life of Mother Teresa, which sits on my video shelf right next to *Up in Smoke* by Cheech & Chong. I have only watched it once, but I remember, distinctly, a scene in which she tells a poor, diseased leper in Calcutta why she's nursing him. "Because I love you," she says. This is not what the priest highlights today. Today, the priest explains that, knowing that there is no guarantee that doing good deeds will get you into heaven, Mother Teresa said, "Do it anyway, no matter what."

Do it anyway, no matter what.

Saturday

Yesterday afternoon, Robert and I went for a swim in a nearby lake where my sister, Laurie, has a camp and so does Shirley's son, Jimmy. Her son Billy is in the process of buying one. In fact, he and Marlous take possession of it this very day. Any moment, they will arrive here at my house, where the previous owner has dropped off the keys.

They will be towing a sailboat, a little two-person job that Shirley bought for her whole family just before she died. "I want to buy something everybody will have fun with," she said thoughtfully as she scanned her checkbook. "I'm thinking about a boat."

"A boat is a great idea," I said. Shirley was always buying presents because she loved to give things away. She asked Billy to find a good sailboat and buy it, and she made monthly payments to him. In Stage One of the Final Dive when she was determined to get her affairs in order, she made me call Billy to ask how much she still owed on it. He played along. He got the precise figure and called back. "One-hundred-fifty dollah!" he said, and we both giggled nervously. Shirley had me write out one of her last checks. Her signature was tiny on the check, one-fifth its normal size, disappearing as surely as she was.

On the phone, Marlous told me that it took six trips to Motor Vehicle to get the boat trailer registered, and Billy made three trips to the hardware store to get the trailer lights connected. Any minute now they will arrive, towing the boat that Shirley bought.

I remembered all of this—her decision to buy a sailboat, the monthly checks, the final one—as I watched a little yellow sailfish cut across the lake yesterday like a sunbeam. I got so choked up just seeing that boat that I had to dive underwater to short circuit a crying jag.

Unity de Montréal
Montréal, Quebec

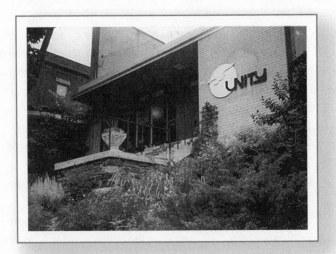

L ately, I have been thinking about borderlands. About the U.S.-
Canada borderland where Shirley lived, and about the borderland between life and death, where I lived with her for seven
months and in some ways, but less and less, I still live. I want to cross
a border for church, so I decide to go to Montréal this Sunday. I call an
acquaintance who sometimes attends an alternative church there. "It's
very diverse," she has told me. "Lots of Haitians." She provides precise
directions, including which traffic lane to be in at crucial moments. This
is the kind of directions I like—the kind I give. I like knowing the best
place to be every second, exactly what landmarks to expect, precisely
how many miles it is from one point to another. I hit the odometer reset
when I leave my parents' house where I've been on overnight Father
Duty. It is 73.1 miles to Unity de Montréal.

At the Trout River border crossing, the customs agent asks me where
I'm going. "Montréal," I answer. "Why? What's in Montréal?" he
responds, aggressively. This startles me. Usually, customs agents ask me

if I'm bringing firearms into Canada or simply wave me through. "I'm going to church," I say, and he immediately signals me on.

The road to Montréal follows a river that winds through small towns named for saints. Here, across the border, the farms are well-kept and productive, unlike the North Country where one by one the farmers go belly up. How can an imaginary line mean so much when the biggest one of all, the border between life and death, is essentially a mirage? A doctor told me when Shirley was dying that the process of decay actually begins before death. You can see the evidence on the person's body and smell it on her breath. For several months, a terrible smell emanated from Shirley's mouth each time she spoke. But just before the Final Dive, it disappeared completely and her breath became sweet, almost childlike. Jimmy and I, who were alone with Shirley at the time, commented on this to each other.

Maybe Shirley's pancreas had completely rotted at that point, evolved past the odor stage as all things do. Yet she was still on the living side of the border. One foot in the grave, I stoically thought as I sat next to her to swab her mouth with a sponge-on-a-stick. When the skin breakdown escalated, I thought, Two feet in the grave. By the time she actually crossed the border, into the mystery, death seemed like a small degree instead of a dramatic finale. I am so absorbed in these thoughts that I barely notice the platoon of cyclists (each bike attached to a baby carriage), or the field in which migrant workers, very black, pick green plants into burlap bags, or even the massive cross atop Mt. Royal. In an instant, it seems, I arrive and park in front of Unity de Montréal.

A black man with a big Caribbean smile and a shaved head greets me at the door. I feel tropical sun in his "*Bonjour*," and as he shakes my hand it transfuses into me. "*Bonjour*," I respond. "*Ça va?*" "*Ahh, bien, bien, bien,*" he says. I'd like to carry on in French, but it is ridiculous to tell him I've run out of gas on the highway, which is the only sentence I have truly perfected in French. Instead, I say, "This is my first time here," and he switches, seamlessly, to English. In the borderland between the U.S. and Québec, most Québécois speak English and almost no Americans, including me, speak French. "Welcome!" he says, and he pats me on the shoulder and gives me a fold-out brochure labeled "Silent Unity Prayer Service."

I enter the church. There are carved wooden wings, a stained glass window depicting the Holy Spirit in the form of a white bird, a podium, flowers, piano. The congregation is mixed in race but unified in age. Everyone is over forty. I only see one young person—a teenage boy, here with his grandmother. Numerous affirmations and prayers are printed on placards all around the room. I focus on the message here at Unity, which seems to center on the power of positivity, potential, and peace. The minister, Yves E. Lafontant, who looks like an elder brother to the man at the door, greets each person by name. The mood is jubilant, as if many friends have run into one another by happy accident.

Yves (everyone calls him Yves) reads the message of the day, which highlights the force of healing, which we can always experience in the moment in our bodies. We sing a few hymns, meditate, listen to a lesson given by a layperson on the power of the phrase "I am," sing some more, and then recite prayers: the Glory Be and the Our Father. Last night, in the middle of the night, I heard my father, Shirley's father, our father's electronic chair crank up into the vertical position, and I went into the TV room. "What're you doing, Dad?" I asked.

"I'm starting my new life," he announced. His mouth, with no teeth, is a sunken black hole.

"Which one is that?"

"The one I had before, when I was independent." He stood unassisted, balanced on his shriveled bow legs.

"Sounds good, but why not start in the morning? It's only three o'clock."

"Time doesn't matter," he said, but time is all he has now, and it tortures him. And he tortures my mother, his primary caretaker, with his constant demands for attention, his relentless complaints, and his frequent verbal jabs. If she retaliates in kind, he snaps, "Hey! You're not the one who's taking a lickin' here."

He has no idea of the lickin' she's taking.

My mother is certain that the state my father is in has been cosmically orchestrated to teach her a lesson. The lesson she must learn, but can't, is how to care for him without resentment. For example, she can't stand emptying the commode. "I'm the number one 'pot wrassler,'" she says, when I ask her how she's doing. She fears she will soon lose her mind if she has to sit with him in front of the TV all day.

"Maybe your lesson is to stand up to him. Just say no," I suggest.

"Oh, I couldn't," she answers.

But somehow, because of all my father and mother are going through, and maybe all Shirley went through, I am willing to say the words to "Our Father" this morning. Forgive us our trespasses as we forgive those who trespass against us, I say.

In the end, we move to the perimeter of the room, make a circle, and sing "Let There Be Peace on Earth." I have sung this hymn in several churches, so I know some of the words. I hold hands with the Haitian teenager and his grandmother. All around the room, there are happy, smiling, singing people. I am singing, too, but tears drip from the ends of my eyelashes. I don't wipe them away. I am an important part of the peace circle, and I simply can't let go.

On my way home, I think about the borderland between life and death (where I lived with Shirley) and the borderland between death and life. Her death and my life. My churches dot this foreign landscape, which I didn't even know I was lost in. I lurch from church to church, I think, and it makes me giddy. Sometimes I imagine I am halfway across a desert, looking for fresh water and God.

New York Presbyterian Church
Queens, NY

Maybe because of the French last week and the Hebrew before that, I arrive at the conclusion that I have been listening to entirely too much English on my crazy path to peace, and I decide to go to a church in which I will not understand one stinking (to use one of Shirley's last words) thing. This is easy because I am in New York City—Queens, actually, theoretically the most racially diverse place on the planet. I am visiting my buddy Marietta from the hippie daze in Boston.

We spend the afternoon basking on the beach at Robert Moses State Park and then, for kicks, we smoke the joint her hairdresser has given her as a fiftieth birthday present and listen to CDs of the classical choir in which she sings. We place a two-hundred-year-old icon of the Blessed Mother, which Marietta has just purchased in Greece, on her piano and stare at it as we listen. Both the music and Blessed Virgin become more vivid in the marijuana haze. I feel blessed myself as I fall asleep on the couch under the protective eyes of Mother Mary.

In the morning, just before I leave her apartment, I speak to Marietta, uninterrupted, for five intense minutes about Shirley's final days—a little burst inspired, I think, because she didn't ask. Remembering how the turf was laid over Shirley's grave within hours so there was not even a seam in the green cemetery lawn, I conclude by saying, "I think Shirley must be farther away now."

"Life yanks you away from many things, including grief," Marietta says. And then she adds, "Thank God."

I nod. Grief, like life, ends, and there's not a damn thing you can do about it.

Still, moving on seems a little disrespectful to Shirley.

I hurry through the slicing rain to the Presbyterian Church of New York, which has just recently been built by Queens Koreans. One rainy day when we sat on the sun porch last summer, Shirley, out of nowhere, said, "It really doesn't matter if I die. It really doesn't." I looked up from the book I was reading and said, "I know." We stared into each other's eyes for several seconds, and later we agreed that we had experienced a great moment of truth. We were proud of the courage with which we faced it. I remember this as I turn the corner, jump the rain puddle, and move toward the church, which looks industrial strength and post-apocalyptic, with its straight lines, concrete, metal railings, no frills.

Maybe one-hundred feet into a large corporate-like entrance hall is an information desk at which two people sit. I inquire about the service, but neither person speaks English. They point me to an office in which two Korean men talk. One has permed grey hair, lifted into a high pompadour, and the other has what my ESL students charmingly call "normal Korean-uncle hair." The service, they tell me, is upstairs. "It's all in Korean," the pompadoured man says. "We have an English service at ten." But I want to go upstairs. I want to hear believers speaking in tongues. Words are just a borderland before the place of no words, I think.

A few days ago, back in the borderland where Shirley lived, I drove down her dirt road for the first time in two months, and I walked around her garden. Early last summer, she weeded every day, and I loaded the weed corpses into her wheelbarrow and dumped them on the compost heap. This year, the weeds are suffocating her flowers. Garden gone, I thought as I backed away from the harsh chaos and circled the house.

The smell of fresh cut grass, grass blood, was very faint.

A woman hesitantly hands me a church program, all in Korean, and I enter a room painted grey and white. The wooden pews quickly fill with small, graceful women in conservative dresses and black-haired men in suits. There is minimal decoration: a highly stylized pipe organ, a podium with pink flowers in front of it, several minimalist thrones spaced across the front, and a video screen on which the minister's face is projected during the service. To the left is a huge choir whose members wear blue and white robes. The service begins with three hymns powerfully performed by the choir and the congregation. A conductor leads us, the audience, with a baton and every person rests a leather-bound hymnal on the built-in book holder on the pews. After the singing, a solemn-faced man recites a prayer. He speaks dramatically, like an English actor doing Shakespeare, though I notice on the video monitor that only his mouth moves—not his shoulders, head, or eyes. I try to listen for the inner meaning of this prayer, and the prayer that follows, and the Bible reading, and musical interlude. A different man delivers a passionate sermon in which, periodically, he yells, stomps his foot, or points his finger skyward. Near its end, he breaks into English for a moment, and I am yanked back into my body. His words are so unexpected that they instantly imprint on my memory:

> Are you happy? Are you really happy? Do you know who is
> your master, your king? Do you know where you're going
> now? Where is your destination?

I feel compelled to answer because your own language makes that demand on you. Yes and no is the answer to each question. All my life I have harbored a secret fantasy that I will one day hear an unfamiliar language and be instantly and unexplainably able to understand it. Now, just as strongly, I want to be free of any language at all.

Of the hundreds of people in the congregation, I am the one and only non-Asian. It makes me think that the minister saw me here, switched to English just for me, and I wish he hadn't. If I could speak Korean, I'd have a question for him, I think, feeling my father rise up in me: "Brother, do you know *your* destination?" I would ask.

Saturday

The day after tomorrow, about five in the morning, we leave for New Mexico. Robert will drive with me, the dog, and the cat in my Dodge Colt Vista. The last two months have disappeared into a time warp. Last week, I heard a science show on the radio about going back in time. Scientists want to build a rocket ship that can beat the speed of light in order to go back a fraction of a second. They should come here, to the North Country, instead. All you have to do is be here and time goes away.

For example, these whole two months, I have not seen my nephew Jimmy, who lives here, except once at Shirley's burial. This seems impossible to both of us. When Shirley was sick and dying, we spent nearly every day together, often all day. I felt fused to Jimmy. We went crazy places, sitting at the kitchen table while Shirley vanished from the next room. Once, Jimmy, Julie, and I tried to recall the Ten Commandments and the Seven Deadly Sins. Once, we had a contest to see who could hold his/her breath the longest, a contest inspired by the unnervingly long pauses Shirley took before and after each respiration. I watched my nephew Jimmy drop water into Shirley's mouth with a syringe. It paralyzed me with love to see him dip the tiny pink sponge-on-a-stick, provided by Hospice, into fresh, cold water for Shirley to suck on when all she wanted was fresh water and God.

At the beginning of Stage Two of the Final Dive, when Shirley was revving up to disappear into the next world or maybe just into death, she spent about twenty-four hours telling us all—in her incoherent, agitated state—to go away, leave her alone. We couldn't and didn't. Instead, we took thirty-minute shifts at her bedside. Once, when Jimmy's shift was over, he came into the living room, where we were all gathered. The Christmas tree lights were on. "Did she say anything?" we tensely asked, because we all desperately wanted words from Shirley.

Jimmy sat down on the couch. He has a quiet, gentle voice. "Yeah. She said, 'Go home.' And she said, 'Get out of here,' and she said, 'Go away.'" He was so matter of fact about it that we all howled. Jimmy still goes to Shirley's house every week on his day off to cut the grass, and check the mouse traps, the heating system, the water pump. But in September, he and Lisa will go to Jamaica, where they will marry on the beach at Ocho Rios. They plan to buy a house closer to Jimmy's job. They are moving on. Moving away.

How did I let my whole summer go by without seeing Jimmy?

Where have I been?

Soon, I will leave the North Country. I know I will never see my father alive again. He and Shirley are the family pioneers into the next world. It is raining. Again. The living room is dark with only a dreamy light coming in from outside. And inside, only the flicker of my Shirley candle.

North Country Church of Spiritualism
Malone, NY

On my last day in the North Country, I park on Raymond Street, one long block from the fairgrounds where Glen Campbell and Tanya Tucker will soon perform. The Grange Hall is a general gathering place where the Masons meet on the first and third Tuesday, the Grange meets on the third Saturday, the Franklin Theater Group is currently presenting a play, *The Housekeeper,* on the weekend nights, and the Spiritualist church assembles today.

The building itself is on the skids. Paint peels off the wooden front porch, the light fixture is rusty, four scraggly geraniums shrivel in the window box, and the lawn has run totally amok with tall white-flowered weeds. It looks as bleak as I feel after overnight duty with my father. I watch a woman with a shoulder tattoo and a puffy eighties haircut emerge from the hall, slip into a Chevy Lumina, and drive away. This leaves just two cars in the vicinity at nine minutes to show time.

I enter a large empty room with several throne-like chairs, probably placed to signify the four directions for the Masons. Thrones are big in churches, which I find hilarious. There is a painting of a waterfall and a small stage set with wicker furniture, obviously for the play currently in production. A little girl seems excited to see me and scampers downstairs to advise some adult of my arrival. I choose a seat and pick up the information folder that has been placed on the chair. I read through the Declaration of Nine Principles, particularly startled by numbers four and five:

4. We affirm the existence and personal identity of the individual continue after the change called death.
5. We affirm that communication with the so-called dead is a fact scientifically proven by the phenomena of Spiritualism.

Before I truly absorb this, a woman about my age arrives to greet me, and I ask her how the Spiritualist church came to Malone. "We lost a grandchild," she says. "We just couldn't make sense of it, and we looked for some kind of explanation, some meaning. After a while we found a Spiritualist church in Swampscott, Mass. The minister there helped us." They formed their own group, and it's growing. Usually thirty or forty people attend on Sunday. Several arrive, and she leaves to greet them.

If you think about it, hardly anybody truly believes in direct communication with the dead. The forty people, plus or minus, who show up here, more than any other church I've been to, are probably drawn in because the pain of losing someone close has pushed them past more traditional religious systems. Spiritualists do not accept that the relationship between themselves and their loved ones can be completely and unapologetically shattered. They don't accept that death is intractable.

I glance up at a sign hanging on the front wall. "No Smoking in Hall," it says, but I misread it, thinking it says "No Smoking in Hell." You can burn in hell, but you can't smoke, I am thinking, and I let out a bleat of laughter. Embarrassed, I glance around to see if anyone has heard, and there, seated right behind me, is Patty, one of Shirley's Hospice nurses, and Jennifer, her Hospice social worker. I am thrilled to see them—war buddies seen unexpectedly far away from the battlefields, after the dead have been laid to rest. Quickly, we catch up. Hospice of the North Country is swamped. Lots of folks are dying. "Do you have room for one more?" I ask, thinking of my father, and they nod. Hospice never says no to the dying.

During the opening prayer, the hymn, and the healing service, I muse on the significance of seeing Hospice workers at the Spiritualist service. They are in the death business; they perform the art of helping people die. They must know more about death than anyone else, except, of course, the ones who pass on. I try to imagine what people pass on to. Not heaven, I don't think. A state of pure potential? A limbo-land to rest up in before the next incarnation? I used to believe in such things, but watching Shirley die, a little idea took hold of me, and, like cancer of the pancreas, it spread. The idea is: there's nothing after this. This idea still makes me feel faint, yet I do not get up and move toward one of the eight folding chairs at the front of the room, where Spiritualist volunteers perform personal, hands-on healings which look to me like Reiki treatments. The healers wash their hands with Handiwipes after each person.

A speaker is introduced, a local woman who recounts a tragic tale of losing her fourteen-year-old son, who was hit by a truck and killed. In the wake of that, everything in her life fell apart: her marriage failed, her finances crashed and burned, and no matter how she tried, she could not compute the loss of her beautiful, beloved child. Her religious faith and her church could not help her. Nothing relieved her of her debilitating grief. But then she found the Spiritualists and learned through experience, she says, that her son still *was*, somewhere and somehow else, in spirit, and she put her life, a complicated puzzle, back together again. She ends by relating a proverb from Africa that helped her make the transition from doubting her former religion to believing in Spiritualism: "If you think your God is made of wood and you learn that it is not, do not throw out your God."

And then it's time for "Messages from the Spirit," a feature of every Spiritualist meeting. Today's medium is Freda Gladle, who lives about one-hundred miles away. Energetic, trim, and in her sixties, she wears a long red dress and an embroidered white sweater. To get us in the right frame of mind to receive her psychic messages, we sing "Zippity Doo Dah" at top volume.

Freda Gladle launches in without preamble. I settle back to listen, suspiciously. Each message begins with the words, "If I'm looking at you right here in the spirit sense..." and often finishes with something like, "I see a grandfather figure who wants you to take better care of yourself." Generic, all-purpose messages from the spirit, suitable for all. She goes up and down the rows with a message for each person. I am not impressed.

When she is only two people away from me, though, just in case, I corral my doubts. Doubt is a force to be reckoned with, and I don't want to blow my chance of receiving a message if one is actually available for me this day. "Be open to the spirit. Be open. Be open," I repeat to myself as the medium comes nearer.

"If I'm looking at you right here in the spirit sense," says Freda Gladle to me, "I see a woman. She's your sis...no, she's a little old to be your sister. Maybe your aunt. No, wait, she says she's your sister." She looks at me. "Do you have a sister who's deceased?" I nod. Tears flood into my eyes as if my reservoir of agony has truly burst the dam. "She's tall—not quite as tall as you. And she's thin—not thin enough for her, though. She always wanted to be thinner. Never accepted what she was. And she had problems with her hands."

Freda Gladle lifts her hands precisely the way I saw Shirley do a hundred times after arthritis set in, when she would say, "If my hands hold out, I'll be fine." Even my mother can imitate this gesture exactly. By now, my concentration is so complete that I think Freda Gladle is the only person in the whole wide world.

"She says to tell you that she came to you three days after she died, but she couldn't get through. She tried, but you couldn't hear her. She says to tell you that she is fine. Just fine. She is happier now than she's ever been; it's better for her than it was when she was here, alive. And she says it's time for you to stop grieving. You have grieved enough. Everything is fine." Freda Gladle touches my shoulder and moves on to the next person. I can hardly breathe.

Could it be? Could it be?

Just say yes, some part of me insists. What more will it take to make me believe?

Just say yes.

The rest of the service—the announcements and the final blessing— dim. When it's over, I take time getting up out of my chair. Jennifer touches my arm. "I'm glad you got to talk to Shirley," she whispers.

That night, when I tell my mother what happened, she gasps and covers her mouth with her fingers. She is absolutely certain that the message is real. I repeat the story for my father because my mother asks me to, and because I want him to know that everything will be fine, just fine, once the doors to the Great Beyond open and he finally hobbles through.

Saturday

All across the country, state by state, I notice, for the first time—even though I have often made this drive—the churches by the side of the highway. Churches are everywhere. Steeples and storefronts. There are billboards, too. Some say "JESUS" with no explanation. Others say "LET JESUS INTO YOUR HEART" or give some website (www.UGOTME JESUS) or quote the Bible. And when my Dodge Colt Vista breaks down in Tucumcari, New Mexico, and we have to rent a car to take the dog, cat, and stuff the last one-hundred-seventy-five miles, I happen to turn the rental-agency card over and on the back it says:

> If I can help please give me a call. The GREATEST CALL I've made was to BE SAVED. It's as simple as A-B-C.
>   A - Admit you're a sinner.
>   B - Believe that Jesus is the Son of God.
>   C - Confess your sins and CALL on the name of the
>   Lord for salvation,
> for whoever does (this includes YOU) shall be saved.
> —Rom. 10:13.

I read it over again wondering why religions are so intent on saving the faithless. I think the faithful are unnecessarily threatened by the faithless.

Long drives, especially in hot cars, make you think. The strangest things become topics for deep meditation. For example, on this trip, Robert and I discuss, for hours, the various versions of highway signs that warn about ice on bridges. Some, like New York state's, are informative: "Bridge freezes before roadway." Others are noncommittal: "Bridge may be icy." Still others place the responsibility squarely on the driver: "Watch for ice on bridges." We speculate on how and why the highway sign people choose their words. In Oklahoma, we have a heyday with "Don't Drive into Smoke," and in New Mexico, when I am giddy about getting home and the open space, I laugh out loud to see the mysterious "Gusty winds may exist."

But there are long, long periods, hours out of every day, when we don't talk, or more correctly, yell, at all over the roar from the four wide-open windows, when I think about the "message from the spirit" that I received, in theory from Shirley, in the Grange Hall a few days ago. I wonder if it's true that death is just "a change" and if the individual consciousness carries on (Principle Number Four). I wonder if Shirley came to see me three days after she died, and if so, why I didn't, or couldn't, feel her presence. I wonder, if she did come, how she came. What was her form? Was she a thought, a dream, a feeling? Or maybe at some point back then I looked at the white December snow of the North Country and thought it was beautiful, and that was Shirley and I just didn't know it.

Shirley's memorial service was on the third day, if I count from Monday. On that Thursday, I got up early to try to write a eulogy. Father Go-Fish, for no apparent reason, did not welcome the idea of anyone giving a eulogy for Shirley, but my niece Julie prevailed, and the great honor of giving one fell to me because I thought I could do it. I thought I could speak about Shirley out loud at her funeral, and none of her kids thought they could. But when I woke up that morning, that Thursday, I felt inadequate and incompetent. The night before, Julie had suggested that I say something about Shirley's spirituality, something about the contemplative life she led. I felt obligated to take her advice, so I will never know what I would have said if left to my own emotional devices.

I wrote something, and in the car on the way to the church, I re-copied it, printing big and skipping lines; then I read it out loud to Robert, who was driving. I needed to recite it at least once so I would not be hearing it for the first time at the funeral, but I kept breaking down. Kept moving the looseleaf paper away so my tears would not drown the words and make them unreadable.

During Shirley's funeral, after the priest's abortion section and after his long tirade about "Little Timmy," a child who tragically drowned, and after he repeatedly called my sister "Mrs. Shirley," he said, "This is the time when we normally bless the body, but... uh...somebody wants to say...something." I got up, out of the pew. I had to walk past Shirley's coffin to get to the podium in front, and when I did I ran my hand, palm down, about six inches above it, all along the length. To me, it was a strange gesture, as if I were pitting my magic against the funeral priest's. I felt for a passing moment like a witch, and he, who still wears the bowl haircut popular among priests of the Dark Ages, was my sworn enemy.

Was that the moment Shirley tried to contact me? Was I too involved in my own private ego battle with the funeral priest to notice?

On the drive out west, I remember looking out over all the "Good People" (as the funeral priest constantly repeated) in the church, giving my eulogy for my sister. I mull over every moment of that third day, thinking about the message I got from Freda Gladle in the Grange Hall: she says you've grieved enough. She says she's fine. Just fine.

Was that really a message from my sister?

What have you got to lose if you believe? I ask myself as we speed into the sunset.

It seems that I, who can and do take the flying leap in a million different ways, lose heart before takeoff when it comes to believing. This is what I'm learning: it takes more than confidence or courage to believe. It is a paradox. It takes belief to believe.

Church of Scientology
Albuquerque, NM

When I open my eyes, the intensely blue New Mexico morning visible through my skylight looks like a color-field painting. I study it with a feeling of deep contentment. The summer in the North Country is behind me now, and already I can see that part of the web in a different light.

For example, I see this: being the black sheep in the family, the sixties hippie complete with every troublesome accoutrement, I always felt terribly misunderstood. Even in the midst of harsh family judgments, though, I knew there was good inside me because Shirley saw it. My sister Mary said in a letter that Shirley "found beauty in strength of character, compassion, and self-sacrifice, and she was very good at finding those things in the least likely individuals," which is all true. Shirley saw into people like me, and it was healing. When she got sick and I went to her, though, I was suddenly transformed into the family angel, and I became hesitant to admit the darkness still inside me that no one seemed to see or even remember anymore. This darkness included the numbness that I let set in with Shirley, my loss of faith, and the deadness I feel (despite both our efforts) about my father.

I went to say goodbye forever to him the night before I left. I sat on the TV room couch next to his recliner. The room smelled vaguely of urine. My father's voice had faded to a whisper, and the bones in his hands seemed ready to push through his skin. "Dad," I said, "I want to tell you that I appreciate all you've done for me." And I truly do: his decades of hard work at a job he despised to support a family of eight. The lessons he taught me about keeping my word, being honest, and (to use a West Pointism) standing up for what I stand for. And for the stories and for teaching me the value of storytelling.

"I know you do," he answered.

There was a little pause then, but I did not add "I love you," even knowing it was the very end. Neither did he. Instead I touched his shoulder and said, "Have courage, Dad." Driving away, back to my little house just seven miles up the mountain, I sobbed so violently that I had to pull to the side of the dirt road. "You hurt me so much," I said out loud in the darkness. I never understood why and I never will, but I know that my father's complete rejection twisted me up inside and ultimately convinced me that there was something fundamentally wrong with me—*something absolutely fundamental*—and I have spent most of my life trying to prove it, hide it, or make up for it. This is the power a father wields. I wish mine had wielded his with a little more care. I do. But then I think of his father, who wouldn't even talk to him in the bakery, and I cry even harder. For him. It is such a tangled, tangled web.

Lucky for me, I had Shirley. I went to her last June, I'm sure now, because I needed to reconnect to the power of love. I needed to believe in it and learn to give it to someone who had hurt me. And I needed to help Shirley learn to receive it. Interestingly, though, she and I never talked about the blank years because, once I was there, they disappeared. Gone.

A memory: very near the end, when Shirley reached the point where she no longer had the strength to stand up, we both had to face the fact that the need for adult diapers was not only looming in the future but actually upon us. Shirley, a nursing home veteran, was upset about this. Hospice supplied the Depends and we waited. Late one night, during Stage One of the Final Dive, I heard Shirley whimpering in her bedroom, and I went in. "I'm gonna go," she said, and I thought, My God! Now? I thought, because I was still in the naive state about death, that she had decided it was the right moment for her to die. My sister Laurie was sleeping on the couch, and I ran into the living room to wake her. "Laurie! Laurie! Shirley's gonna go! Get Julie!" Our niece had just arrived and was asleep upstairs. Laurie tore off. "Julie! Wake up! Shirley's gonna go!" Before they got back to the room, it became clear that Shirley just meant she was going to pee. We all howled. "I thought she meant she was going to die!" I kept repeating. We laughed more. But later, Shirley said privately to me, "You know, I worried and worried about this, but if you just relax and let go, then it's gone, gone away forever, easy as that." She seemed so serene I was sure she was speaking metaphorically.

The blank years, the numbness, was like that, too. We relaxed and let them go, and they just disappeared.

So many things seem simple, looking back. This is the power of love.

I climb out of bed, have my coffee under the mulberry tree, and take off. Destination: the Church of Scientology. Almost thirty years ago, I read *Dianetics* by L. Ron Hubbard, the founder of the Church of Scientology. I was in Miami then, waiting tables on Key Biscayne when another waitress, an older woman of twenty-seven, told me flat out that I would increase my tips by becoming a Scientologist. I went to the Scientology headquarters, where a young man relentlessly bullied me into saying, "I need help." When I did, he sarcastically replied, "Thank you." I never went back. I only lasted six months in Miami anyway, and then I headed north to Montréal in my '62 Plymouth Valiant with the push-button transmission.

The receptionist leads me upstairs to a small room on the second floor. There are eight chairs there, a podium facing them, and a boom-box. The one decorative touch is the "Creed" on the wall, twenty-three core beliefs that seem to be a sci-fi inspired hybrid of politics and utopianism. I am alone in the room long enough to read not only the Creed but the whole "Welcome to Scientology" booklet, which includes a brief history of Scientology, a biography of L. Ron Hubbard (who wrote two-hundred sci-fi novels in addition to beginning his own religion), a dictionary of Scientology terms (of which my personal favorite is "thetan" for human being), and a prayer that closes every service.

Finally, a woman named Johnnie arrives, apologizes for being late, and places a big book with gilded pages on the podium. She starts with a quote from L. Ron Hubbard about the nature of personal integrity:

> What is true for you is what you have observed yourself, and when you lose that, you have lost everything. What is personal integrity? Personal Integrity is knowing what you know, and what you know is what you know, and to have the courage to know and say what you have observed. And that is integrity and there is no other integrity.

It goes on. The word "observed" is repeated over and over again, and it gets increasingly convoluted. Johnnie asks the only other thetan in the audience, a biker, and me to respond. He comments that we should only believe what we have personally observed. I say that this places far too much emphasis on vision. Vision is tricky, I say. It's personal and culture-bound. It doesn't automatically equate with the truth. I'm about to recommend a book on the deception of the visual media when I notice that the minister's eyes have glassed over. I shut up. The minister and the biker both nod pleasantly.

Johnnie proceeds to the sermon section, which she reads directly from the words of L. Ron Hubbard. The topic today is the "Causes of Departure." In Scientology terms, to depart, especially with gusto, is called "blowing off." People blow off because of their own "overts" (actions they do which transgress their own moral boundaries) or "withholdings" (things they should have said or done but didn't). Research has proven, Johnnie reads, that people are not less but more prone to blow off if they're treated well.

I think about the serious pain Shirley suffered for months without looking for another, better doctor. And the way she stopped taking her vitamins and alternative medicines, post-Paul, after her surge into health. And the way she happily stepped off the edge into that Final Dive, her flying leap into the void. I think my sister had unwavering faith that she was on the right path, the one leading to Death.

She wasn't blowing anything off.

Friday

After my Shirley candle sputters out twice due to wax build-up, I decide to clean it up, using the technique I learned from the monks at Christ in the Desert monastery. This involves soaking the candle-glass in hot water and then digging out the softened wax with a table knife. I know it is a risk, considering the long crack in the glass, but I intend to be gentle. I have to do something because the wax inside has formed a deep hole that simply snuffs out the life of the flame.

When I go to work with the knife, though, the red glass from the Sanctuario in Chimayo breaks into two jagged pieces. They fit perfectly but cannot hold together.

Things fall apart.

I take two fat blue rubber bands off my organic broccoli, stretch them around the glass, and drop in a new votive candle. It works, though little lines of molten wax seep through the crack and raise a translucent scar on my tabletop.

Later, I talk to my sister Joanie, who is in the North Country again to take care of our father. He is slipping fast and has been in the hospital where they have siphoned two liters of fluid out of his chest. He is scheduled to come home within hours, and when I talk to her, Joanie is awaiting the delivery of a hospital bed, which will replace my father's recliner. My father can't stand up anymore. Everything but the TV and a couch for visitors has been cleared out of the TV room to make space for the bed.

Intensely, I start to explain to Joanie about folding a sheet into thirds, lengthwise, and putting it crossways on the bed. This, I say, is the best way to roll a bedridden person over. It's torture on the back to try to lift a human body, even a skinny old man. My father, who weighed one-hundred-and-seventy pounds his whole life, now weighs ninety. Shirley, before ascitis (the pooling of fluid in the abdomen) set in, was down to ninety-three pounds, and it was still a terrible strain to move her. "It's because you have to lean so far forward," I tell Joanie. I tell her to be sure to crank the bed up to the right height, and about the sponges-on-a-stick for mouth swabbing and the fleece for the pillows and cutting the straws in half to cut down on the hard work of sucking and…

I push her to make "the parental unit," as I call my father and mother, sign up with Hospice. Just a few days ago, I found out, by relentless grilling, that my mother, who was raised dirt-poor and has spent her life trying to forget it, associates Hospice with soup kitchens and welfare. "It's not for destitute people," I tell her. "Hospice is for everyone."

A sick feeling, very sick, has centered itself in my stomach. Thinking about the end of life, about caring for those who have arrived there, seems much more overwhelming when I imagine Joanie doing it than it did when I was the primary caretaker myself. I feel intense dread on her behalf.

"Don't worry. I'll just do it," she says.

"It will seem really normal, really natural," I offer.

But from outside of it, from miles and months away, I finally feel the strain of having been there, done that.

"The horror, the horror," I say.

And we both chuckle.

Unification Church of New Mexico
Albuquerque, NM

On the day before Robert left, we drove to Wal-Mart to buy bargain basement items for the tiny apartment I have rented in the Jemez Mountains, near the Indian reservation where I am about to start my new career as a ninth grade English teacher. We passed the Unification Church of New Mexico whose sign invites all passersby to Sunday service at eleven. I decided to go. Images, perhaps inaccurate, of the Reverend Moon arrived in my mind. Group weddings held in baseball stadiums.

When I pull up and park, it's twenty to eleven and there are only four cars in the tiny lot; by five to eleven, no one else has arrived and there isn't a single pedestrian in sight. I get out of the car to study three closed doors. A fourth door is up a flight of stairs. A fluorescent light burns on the second floor, so I climb the stairs and knock loudly on the door. No one answers, although I wait a full minute.

I go back downstairs and scan the building carefully. Bells are mounted beside each door, and now I notice mailboxes, too. I expand my visual range to incorporate the whole parking lot, and for the first time I notice a large "FOR SALE" sign on the wooden fence. That's when I realize that this is not a church any more; the Sunday service sign is just a leftover. The building has been broken into apartments, and the four cars in the lot obviously belong to the tenants.

I stand confused in the blazing July sun at two minutes to eleven and then make a snap decision: today I will go to the UNM library and look up Clifford Geertz's definition of religion. Ever since it emerged unsummoned in my mind on my first Sunday, I have wondered about its accuracy.

The library, built more than a hundred years ago, is a church in itself, if you ask me, and I am fluent in its rituals. I sit at a computer, do a search by key words, and find the article in the periodicals room downstairs. Geertz says that religion

> is a system of symbols which acts to establish powerful, pervasive, and long-lasting moods and motivations in men by formulating conceptions of a general order of existence and clothing these conceptions with such an aura of factuality that the moods and motivations seem uniquely realistic.

Well, I think as I settle back in the big armchair on the landing, I simplified it but I certainly had the gist. I remember reading this definition for the first time twenty-three years ago and being supremely shocked. I had always assumed that religion was real—"really real," as I paraphrased it back in January.

Thinking it over, I decide there are only two reasons for religion. One: we invent religion out of fear. Two: we invent religion to express what's really, really there.

The spirit.

Friday

I have read that after a person dies, in certain Native American cultures like the Navajo, his or her name is never mentioned again. If you want to speak about the deceased, you say "that person who used to live here," because to use a name is to call up a spirit who wants to rest elsewhere. I have been thinking about this because I wonder if I am possibly breaking the cosmic rules that separate life and death by speaking about Shirley in some way. I say her name to someone, probably every day, more than when she was alive, when she simply *was*, way upstate, down at the end of the dirt road. Then, all those years, she was simply Shirley, who *was*.

Now she isn't, but I think about her more, about her life and death, her graces and shortcomings, her beauty and her pain. I wonder if I do this because I can only reflect on what I had in my sister by acknowledging what I've lost, or if the going-over I do of her life is a way to repave memory traces so I won't lose her completely.

When my father was in the hospital the first time this summer, a nurse asked him how many children he had, and he answered, "Six daughters, but we lost one recently." I thought then about the verb "to lose," about why it has come to describe the helplessness brought on by the death of a loved one. When you lose something, it's gone forever; you don't know where it is, and you have no hope of finding it ever again. When Shirley died, we all lost, but the loss increases if she slips out of memory, too. So I light my Shirley candle, picture her face, remember her laughter. For the first time in my life, I have hung a picture of my five sisters and me on the wall by my bed. I am in contact with my four remaining sisters far more often than ever before in my life. In the past, several years could go by and we would not speak.

When I arrived back in New York in June a year ago, right after Shirley was finally diagnosed, my next older sister, Janet, was already there. She had rushed to Shirley from Calgary. For thirty years, she has been a palliative care nurse, and she wanted to see Shirley, establish and supervise her care, be there. When Shirley asked her why she had scrambled so to get there, Janet said, "Because you taught me how to love."

Of course, Shirley didn't get it, but I did.

On my first night in the North Country, I drove Janet back to our parents' house from Shirley's. We bawled nonstop, but suddenly, midway back to Malone, we began to talk about our own relationship, which has always been distant and uneasy. I pulled to the side of the road and stopped the car, maybe two-hundred feet from our parents' driveway. "Janet," I sobbed, wiping snot away from my nose with the back of my hand, "I'm so sorry for punching you in the stomach." It happened in the backseat of the car on a long trip to Rochester. I must have been eight years old because Laurie was about three or four, sitting in the front seat on my mother's lap. Janet was twelve. I felt such a surge of rage and bitterness, arriving out of nowhere, that I pounced on Janet across the back seat and socked her as hard as I could, right in the belly. Janet doubled over. My father had to pull to the side of the road so she could throw up.

I have wanted to apologize for this for my whole life.

My mother tells me, in an offhand moment, that in seventy years of marriage, my father has never, not once, apologized for anything.

Later, I tell Shirley about it, and she says, "Maybe that's the good that will come out of this."

"What good?"

"Maybe the sisters will find each other."

Diamond Way Tibetan Buddhist Center
Albuquerque, NM

I wake up wondering if I've got religion after all. It seems clear this morning that each church I've attended, each organized religion I've experienced, has, oddly, led to something fading away rather than collecting into a solid core of belief and faith. I thought I would rebuild my faith, but instead I am shedding. Maybe what's left after all the shedding is my religion.

I get out of bed and dig through the pile of papers on my kitchen table to find my copy of Geertz's article, "Religion as a Cultural System." Heading it off is a quote by Santayana:

> The vistas [each religion] opens and the mysteries it propounds are another world to live in; and another world to live in—whether we expect ever to pass wholly over into it or not—is what we mean by having a religion.

I think back to my seven tarot years when I lived, day and night, in the alternate reality of archetypes and symbols, dream interpretation and mystical connections. It was an excellent world to inhabit. It provided a framework big enough to make sense of each passionate emotion, unruly thought, or irrational action. But then I fell from grace somehow, just like Adam and Eve. I passed wholly out of it. Did I shed a belief system then, enter another one, or just get lazy? I can't even remember now. Maybe the alternate reality became too tight, and I squirmed out of it like a snake in the spring. Or maybe I began to doubt. Back then, I began every morning with a cabalistic aphorism: I will regard every circumstance of my life as the direct dealing of God with my soul. Did God send me away from religion, then? Did God wait a while, and then send Leroy?

I feel dreamy and cosmic this morning. I skip coffee and have hot lemon water instead because it seems more pure. I am going to the Diamond Way Tibetan Buddhist Center, which holds a Sunday meditation at one o'clock. For no apparent reason, I have several items related to Tibetan Buddhism in my *casita*: a photograph of the Dalai Lama; prayer flags over my entry door; a dramatic black T-shirt picturing the eyes of Buddha that I purchased after observing some traveling Tibetan monks create (and then destroy, because nothing is permanent) a sand painting; and one of the brass funnels that these same monks used to pour the sand into place. I find a strange comfort in these objects.

The Diamond Way Tibetan Buddhist Center is a little house, not far from Nob Hill. I enter what would be the living room if it hadn't been transformed into a meditation room. The hardwood floor is covered with small, hand-woven rugs. Incense burns. There are a few statues of Buddha on the bookshelves. I say hello, remove my shoes, ask permission to use a meditation pillow, and settle onto one of the rugs. Including me, there are seven people.

"What're we going to do today?" asks a mom of three who arrived in a late-model Volvo station wagon.

The host-woman answers, "The sixteenth karmapa."

This turns out to be a guided meditation/visualization in which we imagine the Buddha emanating clear light from his third eye into ours; then red light from his throat into ours; then blue light from his heart into ours. In the temple of tarot, these colors would be yellow, green, and orange, but they would glow from the same places. A few times, I slit my eyes and look around the room. Everyone but me has prayer beads, which click against the floor. A tiger-stripe cat sleeps on the rug near me. Silently, I scratch his ears. When the meditation ends, we all stretch dramatically. Then we sing a long poem called the Invocation:

> OM MA DAG NO CHU TONG PAR JANG
> TONG PAI NGNAG LE YE SHE CHI
> LUNG ME THO JE TENG NYI DU
> TO PAR SHE NGA DU TSI NGA
> LUNG ME KOL WAI DAM TSHIG PAI
> etc. (It continues for forty-six lines.)

I chant along, having no idea at all what story I am telling. In my heart, though, I know exactly what I'm praying for. I want to turn into whatever I will be after the rest of the spiritually obsolete pieces have fallen off.

Then I think of what is left of Shirley: her memory, her children, and her legacy of love.

Friday

At 7:30 in the morning, my friend Whitney and I take a long walk by the river with our three dogs. She asks me how I have responded to doubters who have scoffed at the notion that I thought I could get a sense of a religion from a single visit to its church.

"No one cares enough about what I do to scoff," I reply. But as we walk on, through the red dust, I realize that may not be true. Truthfully, I haven't felt that anyone had the urge to scoff. When I say how I spent seven months with my dying sister who suffered a spiritual crisis which rubbed off on me, I get respect. I treat it very seriously, and so does everyone else. Sometimes I think that's a problem. I should lighten up. Think of this as a great adventure instead of the labors of Hercules.

We come around a bend in the path and see the river. There are birds standing on one leg on a mud bank in the middle, and the water, all riled up from rain, looks exactly like chocolate milk. "So have you found a church you want to go back to?" Whitney asks, quickly adding that she feels a church-need and wonders if I can make a recommendation.

"It's so complicated," I respond. "It all depends on what you want."

"I want...spirituality," she says. "I want to feel it." We walk on a few steps, and she adds, "Maybe the Baptists."

I do not mention that the True Vine Baptist Church was locked up when I went there. We proceed single file through the narrow part of the path. Finally, I say, "Picking a church is huge. It could take fifty or a hundred Sundays or…"

"A lifetime," Whitney supplies.

Then I tell Whitney about the message from the spirit world, the message I received from Shirley at the Spiritualist service, and she stops in her tracks and demands more details. I give her the play-by-play, and she asks me if I believe it. "Well," I hedge, "sort of. But I'm still up in the air about continued consciousness after death."

"I believe in ghosts," she replies, confidently.

She asks me if I remember the third day after Shirley died and I tell her I've been over it and over it, but I can't figure out when, how, or if I missed Shirley's visit. And then, spontaneously, I reveal something else, something I have not told a single person. A few days ago, while I was working at my desk, I had the odd sensation that someone was watching me. Curious, I looked over my shoulder, my eyes moving directly to the photograph of my sisters and me that now hangs on the opposite wall. It looked as if a bright light was shining directly on Shirley.

Shirley was actually glowing.

I felt a knock in my chest, an intense lightening.

"Maybe that was her," I say to Whitney, who is walking ahead of me now through the field of *yerba del manso*. She looks adorable in her floppy sun hat from K-Mart with a flower in the brim.

"It was," she responds.

Islamic Center of New Mexico
Albuquerque, NM

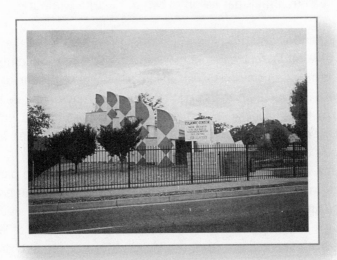

Nobody tells the whole truth about death—or witnessing it. The truth is, it's hard work for the dying person. It's just as difficult getting out as it is coming in. I don't understand how I could have made it to almost fifty and not known this. If there'd been a handbook with specific chapters detailing the gasping for breath, the skin breakdown, or the death smell, would I have read it? I certainly studied the little booklet Hospice provided as if it were the Bible: expect the dying person to tear at his/her clothes, expect excruciatingly long pauses between respirations, expect the worst. But until you're there yourself, you can't know. It is awesome. It is a whole other part of the web, the part that's only lightly attached. I'm glad I went there with my sister. I'm grateful for the experience, for having had the opportunity to see the truth about Shirley dying. At least I knew her truth inside out. But now I am moving away from it. The survivors resurrect somehow, rise up, away from the dead, out of the hole in the ground and the one in their hearts.

This is my twenty-ninth Sunday. Occasionally, around my edges, I feel a little dread about my *Month* ending. This is what I've learned so far: give love, live in the now, trust that all parts of the web of life are equal and necessary. Stop worrying about God and feel His/Her/Its presence everywhere, in every cell and every moment. It's so simple. But sometimes I'm afraid that I won't keep this clarity without my Sunday ritual.

I am thinking about this as I pull into the parking lot of the Islamic Center of Albuquerque, an oddball brown and white building a few blocks north of the airport, just ahead of two government minivans filled with Arab men, perhaps prisoners, in every kind of Middle Eastern garb from the burnoose to djelleba. They tumble out and enter the "MEN ONLY" door. All around me, cars screech into spaces and out climb men of every possible color.

The first woman I see wears all white—veil, blouse, loose pants and high platform shoes with gold stars on them. I ask her if I can enter the mosque without a headdress. "Yes, you can come in," she smiles, but before I get close to the door, a white woman pulls me aside to lend me a scarf which she collects from the backseat of her car. She drapes it over my head, explaining each step. I bend my knees and turn around in the parking lot to give her better access to my head. When she finishes, she looks at me and says, "Very Bedouin." In we go. This woman, Maggie, shows me where to leave my shoes and car keys. "You're not menstruating?" she whispers.

"No," I say.

"Good." She instructs me to sit anywhere and disappears to wash up. There are no chairs of any kind, and the mosque is divided down the center by a curtain about six feet high. I can hear men on the other side, and I see a pair of bare brown feet, cut off at the ankles by the curtain. All through the prayers, little children cross back and forth between the two spaces and once I see a woman move a part of the curtain aside to peek in there.

I drop down among the other women—all ages, all colors—on the burnt-orange industrial carpeting. Many of the women have small children, who stretch out with their heads on their mothers' laps. There are lots of babies, and plastic diaper bags are everywhere. Soon, Maggie comes out of the washroom all in white with her veil clipped tightly under her chin. I feel almost giddy in my (her) Bedouin wrap, looking like I did when I was a kid playing "nuns" and using a Turkish towel for a veil. "This sister has come to observe," Maggie says, introducing me to a few women. They touch my hand, squeeze my fingers, say "Salaam."

Suddenly, from the other side of the curtain, a man sings out, loud and long. "That's the call to prayer," Maggie whispers, and then she explains what will happen here: a section of the Koran will be read in Arabic and English by men on the other side of the curtain; we will bow, prostrate ourselves en masse to the floor three times; prayers will be said. The prayers are the same as you'd find in any Christian church in the world, she says: Give glory to God, God is good. Like that.

Maggie's eyes are very blue, and her skin is even paler than mine.

She is enthusiastic about Islam. "It took the prophet Mohammed twenty-three years to transcribe Allah's direct communication," she says. "By the time Mohammed came along, Christ, as a prophet, at least in the Middle East, was obsolete. The prophets express the times. Christ arrived at a time when physicians were greatly respected, which is why he came as a healer. In Mohammed's day, poets were respected, so he was a poet. The Koran is pure poetry," Maggie says. Then she asks me if I am a member of any religion. "Nope," I say, but then I add, "I was raised Catholic, but..." She nods, points at herself with her thumb, nods again. She asks me why I've come, and I tell her in one sentence about Shirley. "I've been coming to different churches every week since January, waiting to see...if I get the call."

"In Islam, you get the call five times a day," she smiles.

Saturday

I went to Home Depot and, for fourteen dollars, I bought a garden tool with a long wooden handle and a serrated blade. Every evening, after the sun goes down, I use it to hack down the Deadly Nightshade that has grown waist-high in Julie Reichert's back yard. From the dirt there, all sorts of oddities are coughed up: forks and spoons, broken glass, silver coins, and even an Indian arrowhead. I collect them and shove them into tree stumps. I swing my new tool like a golf club, working up a serious sweat. A callus is even developing below my wedding ring. First I chop the weeds, and then I kick them into small piles all over the yard.

There is no clear reason why I took on this chore. The purple flowers of the Deadly Nightshade were lovely, and we had a little path, maybe a foot wide, through their prickers to the clothesline. But I became obsessed, suddenly and without explanation, with getting rid of it all. Like a mercenary, I viciously hack at the thick stems. I gloat over the stalks that stick up everywhere like sharp bamboo spikes, and when new weeds, little plants that grow six inches overnight, spring up, I decapitate them with glee, close to the earth. "Take that!" I sometimes say before I swing the scythe.

Julie Reichert thinks it's all rather amusing.

"You're getting good at chopping," she commented as she watched me go at it last night, "I see you have abandoned the back and forth motion."

"Yeah, it doesn't work," I grunted. "These weeds are ornery." I smashed one with the serrated edge.

Now, in the dim morning glow of my Shirley candle, I'm wondering if this is one more case of slippage between symbols and real life. All through my *Month of Sundays*, I have thought of my doubts as mental weeds corrupting my little patch of spiritual hope. My doubt says, "There is no order in the universe. No hereafter. No meaning. No hope. No point at all."

I gaze out my skylight as dawn arrives. Simultaneously, it dawns on me that I have been thinking in black and white about belief and doubt. I have made an unnecessary assumption: that it's all or nothing. No grey area whatsoever.

I think about the weeds in the back yard. Some are shrinking and turning brown in the piles I've placed here and there; some are already in the compost bin, transforming themselves into something useful. But many are going strong. This is the way it is. The tension comes from the desire to be in total control of the weeds every minute.

If I make a connection between weeds and doubts, as I have been, there's a message here for me. Belief and doubt may be in an eternal tug-of-war, but it's the war, not the doubt, that creates the tension. And I am tired of being the battleground. If there's no battleground, can there even be a war?

Instead of worrying about it, I roll over. My bed is supremely comfortable, and the temperature in the *casita* is perfect. This moment, right now, is all there is.

Eckankar:
Religion of the Light and Sound of God
Albuquerque, NM

I arrive at the strip mall in which Eckankar is located early enough to raid the stash of free literature outside the door. In "What is Eckankar?" I learn that "Light and Sound are twin aspects of God." This Holy Spirit, "known in Eckankar as the ECK, sustains all life." The religion was founded in the 1960s by Paul Twitchell who ascended in 1981, "after years of spiritual training, to become the Mahanta, the Living ECK Master." The Mahanta gives "inner guidance through dreams, Soul Travel, and the Spiritual Exercises of ECK." For this, he gets respected but not worshipped. Currently, the ECK Master is Harold Klemp. In the picture, he looks like a normal guy from the Midwest, an

Alan Alda type with a receding hairline.

Several people enter the storefront church—mostly white, forty and up, more women than men. One elderly couple arrives with a little dog on a leash, which I find charming. This is the first church to which you can bring your dog. I step inside and an elderly man gives me a program. On its cover is the thought for the day: Letting God into Your Life through Patience.

A little burst of happiness explodes inside me like a firecracker because I feel immediately connected to Shirley. If there was one thing she consistently lectured me on, it was patience. Shirley thought I lost out on whole experiences because I impatiently cut them short. She appreciated my ability to do a bang-up job, but she said I cheated myself of the pleasure of making whatever it was as close to perfect as possible, of waiting to see what would happen.

Smiling, I sit in the middle of the three rows of chairs and look around. There are printed placards on the wall, all with quotations of Harold Klemp: "The law of love can carry you to God." "Be awake among the sleeping." "Soul exists because of God's love for it." Several people introduce themselves to me before today's "officiator," David, takes the power chair at the front. He begins with a reading from Harold Klemp's book, *The Slow Burning Love of God:*

> When times are hard some people complain. As they complain about hard times, they shut themselves off from the opportunities that lie within their troubles. Other people have learned to be patient. They look for the lessons within their hardships or troubles.

I expect more, but he makes no comment. Instead, we begin the "Love Song to God," the Hu (pronounced "hue"), an ancient word for God, the chanting of which will lead us to the temple within. If we want to, David says, we can meditate on patience during this song.

He sets the tone by chanting "Hu." Everyone joins in, all sorts of voices. There doesn't seem to be a prescribed length for anyone's Hu, and people begin when they choose to and end when their breath runs out. My own voice comes out at a much higher pitch than I expect. I consciously try to lower it, but it won't drop, so I surrender to the high notes. No sooner do I do that than my voice comes out baritone—lower even than David's. Suddenly, on the screens inside my eyelids, the group Hu becomes visual, like a map or a puzzle in which I can see some pieces missing. I try to fit my voice into the missing places so the group texture will be complete.

The Hu-ing goes on for about five minutes before David ends it and opens the discussion. Several Eckists reveal insights and personal stories related to patience: *impatience*, one person says, is about expectations; it is typically selfish, leads to anger, and prevents the heart from being open enough to experience the Mahanta's love in the moment. Patience lets us see the harmony in cycles; with it, we can recognize patterns and understand timing. Patience is not a restraint but a dynamic opportunity. It's a spiritual practice, David adds, which you don't have to be in a quiet room to do. Having patience to see what unfolds is a way of trusting that there will inevitably be a return to pleasant circumstances. This desire for pleasant circumstances, he says, is a desire for God.

I do not offer anything, though for a second I am tempted to blurt out details of my *Month of Sundays*, about how long I've been at it, how I've stuck with it no matter what, and how, near the end, I do not feel impatient with myself, God, or anyone else. Instead, I happily decide to keep my big mouth shut.

Wednesday

I am packing up to head north to the apartment I rented near the high school. I have collected a few books, a set of sheets, four dishes and a pot into a pile on the table to take out to the car.

When I pick up the first load, I accidentally knock my Shirley candle off the table and it smashes to smithereens on the concrete floor.

My first thought arrives, quick and clear: Geez, Shirley, you'll do anything to get me to sweep the floor.

I stand, mesmerized by the red shards, the blue rubber broccoli-bands, the thousand pieces, scattered in a big circumference, like planets and stars in deep space.

I start to laugh as I stoop down to pick up the big pieces with my fingers and put them into a plastic baggie.

Then I find the broom and commence to sweep. There is a lot of desert sand on my floor, and I have a big pile collected in the dustpan when Julie Reichert appears in my doorway. She has just taken my dog for a walk by the river.

She looks at the mess on the floor.

"I broke my Shirley candle," I explain.

"Your project is ending," she responds, kindly.

True Vine at Five Points Baptist Church
Albuquerque, NM

On my last Sunday, I return to the True Vine where I started out thirty-one weeks ago. I am afraid it will be closed again and I repeatedly call the number in the phone book, but nobody answers. Nervous, I show up early and am thrilled to see people milling outside. I enter the little building next to the church, the one where I found the plaque with the name "Carter" on it that first snowy Sunday in January. It is a small room with maybe ten pews on each side. There is no crucified Jesus. Everyone here is black, all ages. Immediately, two beautiful women come over to introduce themselves to me, and then the Reverend Richardson, a handsome man with a shaved head, a goatee, and a brown suit with a mustard-colored shirt, shakes my hand. Seconds later, the main minister, Reverend Vernon Bobbs, strolls over. I recognize him from his photo, which hangs above a door to the left side of the church. Today, he looks dramatic in his white suit and tie with a black shirt and two-tone black and white shoes. When he shakes my hand and smiles, I see two gold teeth. He is, I think, not much older than I am.

I grip his hand in both of mine, hold it tightly, and summarize my whole story—how my sister died, and I started to go to churches. How I came here first, but the True Vine was locked up. How I have been to thirty other churches since, but here I am, back again, for the grand finale.

"Welcome, welcome," he says.

It crosses my mind that he probably thinks I'm nuts. I watch him vanish into the door below his formal portrait; then I sit down to watch a thin man in a grey suit set up his electric guitar down front. On the pew in the row in front of me is a gleaming saxophone.

The service begins with music. Four female singers gathered below the elevated podium at which Reverend Richardson waits form a cloud of intense gospel music upon which the reverend seems to hover. Guitar rains music down on us, like an electrical storm. Everybody, me too, begins to sway in our pews as the Reverend Richardson revs up. He speaks softly but his passion builds and soon he's yelling out his thanks for all the gifts we have, courtesy of God. I like this kind of worship— belted out to an electric guitar. "Some people say the end is near," Reverend Richardson hollers, his shaved head beginning to glisten. "I think that's good! That's when the Lord is going to come and purge us! What better time could there be to live than at the end? If it's the end, we're gonna get to see the Lord come down and save us! Thank the Lord. Thank you, Jesus! Amen." "Amen!" people yell from the congregation. "But if you wanna be used by God, it's gonna cost you!" Reverend Richardson hollers. "You got to pay."

This is a sobering thought, though I know very well that all things have a price tag, and getting through the Pearly Gates is no exception. Even if you feel that you've paid in full all your life, generated so much love that people call you an angel (like they called Shirley), you get put through the wringer at the end, and that's the way it is. That's life, and that's death. I reflect on this all through the announcements. Today, it turns out, is the anniversary of the True Vine Church. There will be a big celebration starting at three. So many cycles, so much motion, so many beginnings and endings, that I don't know which is which anymore.

The choir is called forward. Boys and men sit in the back row, women and girls in the first three. A teenager with rippling muscles, a tight dress, and a tumble of cornrows lifts up her golden saxophone and blows the hell out of it. The choir belts it out, the guitar reverberates, the saxophone howls, and some people, including me, gyrate and clap. I feel I am tumbling headfirst into the music, and I close my eyes in ecstasy. Is this the spirit? The words we sing are, "I'm determined to walk in love."

Now Reverend Bobbs emerges from the side room. His black robe with white satin crosses on the chest shimmers as if it wants to dance, and it's hard to calm down for the Bible reading. "Do you have a Bible, Sister?" he asks me from the front.

"No."

"Somebody find that sister a Bible!" Reverend Bobbs calls out and one is placed instantly in my hand. We turn to a passage I recognize but can't name—the one about green pastures, like Shirley had on her farm. "When I was a child I spoke like a child." That one. The one that ends with "Now the three remain—faith, hope, and love. But the greatest of these is love."

Absolutely, I see Shirley's face as I read and remember how she exuded love. Not sappy, saccharine, or mushy love. Just plain love. And suddenly, I recall something my sister Mary wrote to me months ago. She said, "I have always remembered 'God is love' from the blackboard in my eighth grade class. I never understood what it meant then, but I do now. Love is the language of God. It is the way He wants us to communicate. I think it was, and is, the presence of God in you, the love in you, that made you give up everything in your life to take care of Shirley." I feel stunned, flooded, remembering that, but I shift my attention back to the True Vine. Since this is my last Sunday, since this might well be the last Bible passage I ever hear, and since I am so lost in Shirley thoughts, tears sting my eyes as I recite the final words, "But the greatest of these is love."

Then the Reverend Vernon Bobbs commences to preach.

His theme is listening. We have to listen close to hear the word of God, and we need to get our lips to say the right words back. His words shift cadence, fall into sound patterns like chords, and then they lift off and he is singing. The guitarist gets up from the front row, straps on his guitar, and does licks behind the Reverend Bobbs.

"When you hear the Lord calling you," Reverend Bobbs croons, "you gotta say, 'I'll go!'" "I'll go!" he wails. "I'll go!" He struts back and forth across the front of the room like James Brown, his robe swirling about his two-tone shoes, instructing us to listen up. Because once you listen with your whole heart, you'll be able to shout it out, too: "I heard you, Lord! I heard!"

I am riveted in this borderland between religion and showbiz. My ears open up, as if they suddenly have better circulation, and the cartilage in them gets hot. Once I read a Bob Dylan quote that went something like this: "It blows my mind that this country could have a president who has never been to the Apollo Theater." I have been there, to 125th Street in Harlem, but I have never been the only white person in a black church. It feels excellent to be here, to lose myself, to surrender to the music, to the words, to the power of the story Reverend Bobbs wants to tell and to the way he tells it, too. I feel transported, high. As if he's read my mind, he yells, "You don't need no Jack Daniels to get high! The Lord will make you high."

"I got a flint rock right here," he bellows, tearing open his robe to show us his heart. "You got one, too. We can all make a spark. We can all spark the fire, the fire of love of Jesus. Don't come here, depending on me to do it for you. You got to do it your own self. You got to light your own fire. That's the only way it works. They got eternal flames for Martin Luther King and President Kennedy," he says. "I got my own eternal flame, right here."

Do I have one? My own flint rock? My own eternal flame?

"If you feel the Lord, come up here!" Reverend Bobbs calls out. "If you feel the Lord, you come up here right now!" he repeats and then to my dismay he points right at me.

Right at me.

His arm is fully extended and I can feel the power of his finger on me, like God and Adam in the Sistine Chapel ceiling, but I don't move. I don't give up that last inch because my mind has inserted itself into the borderland between my swaying body and Reverend Bobbs. My mind will not surrender to this organized religion, to Jesus Christ. And I do not know for certain if what I'm feeling is the Lord, though it sure feels good. Reverend Bobbs points at me for so many consecutive seconds that a few people turn around to look.

I stand still. My heart bangs in my chest and about forty-nine percent of my cells are in a frenzy and want me to take that one step forward. But I don't. I can't. Not specifically toward Jesus. Finally,

Reverend Bobbs moves on to another person, a young woman who does indeed have the spirit. She has just accepted her role as a missionary of Christ and is here with her soon-to-be husband. Reverend Bobbs calls both of them to come down front to receive some premarital counseling.

"Tell him you love him," he instructs the young girl. "Often." He turns to the young man. "Tell her you love her. Every day."

Be kind, do the right thing, walk away if you're tempted to say something hurtful. Walk away if you can't leave that person better off, or at least as good, as they are right now.

"Don't be a henpecked husband," he warns the man.

"Don't try to control the henhouse," he advises the woman.

A few other women, including his wife, I think, and I glance toward one another and erupt in little hoots.

"If you have trouble, come see your pastor. Don't take nothing out on each other."

Near the end of the service, after the collection, Reverend Bobbs turns to me again. "Stand up, Sister," he says. In all the churches I've been to, I have never stood up, not once. But now, at the last possible moment, I am forced to take it: the eyes of the group upon me. A public statement that I am here, in church, looking for God. I stand in the little flowered dress that Shirley made for me, wondering if she can see my white face, blushing red with embarrassment, among those who have the spirit, who believe.

"I'll go!" I said a few minutes ago, along with everybody else. "I'll go!" I said when I got the idea of *A Month of Sundays*. "I'll go," Shirley said at the end of her life. "I want to go to God," she said. Reverend Bobbs retells the story I blurted out to him—about the thirty-one churches. "She was determined to come here," he tells the True Viners. "Now, Sister, you come back. We can save you."

I smile and say thanks.

When it all ends, I slowly cross Bridge Boulevard. My car is in the same lot, the same parking place, that it was when I started out in January. It's nine months since Shirley died. It's the anniversary of the True Vine Baptist Church. It's the end of my *Month*. I am wobbly on my feet. My search for the spirit has worn me plum out.

Saturday

My father died sometime between three and five this morning, at home and in his sleep, just the way he wanted to. Hospice came like they do to check for a heartbeat and to make the death pronouncement. The nurse, Patty, whom I last saw at the Spiritualist service, went into the TV room and put the stethoscope to my father's bony chest. There was not much left of him. He weighed about eighty pounds. She came out into the dining room where my mother and sister Mary waited. "He's a free spirit now," she said.

Robert called me in the morning with the news. Holding my breath, I heard his words. Then I said, "I'll just say what my father said when I told him that Shirley had died: God bless him."

He is flying home.

My mother, by all reports, is doing fair to middling. I imagine she will spend a long time recovering from the stress of the last incredibly sad and difficult year. It's funny how similar it all is—being the caretaker or the dying person. Somehow you hold it all together for however long; then the death occurs, and you fall apart.

I hear little pieces of the story in short phone calls to the four sisters I have left. How my father, a proud man who went down fighting, rattled the bars of his hospital bed for the last day and kept trying to strip off his clothes. He paid a high admission price to the Great Beyond.

My niece Julie, who happens to be in the North Country, told me that Paul, the faith healer, had showed up at my parents' house last week. "He did? How did that happen?" I mumble, shocked. But it doesn't matter. Julie said he came and said a rosary with my parents. He asked them to hold hands and reflect on how they felt about each other in the early years, before illness set in. The years before my mother couldn't hear and my father couldn't project his voice anymore and all they did was bicker. He prayed with them, and Julie said that my sister Mary, who was there at the end, reported that my mother and father stopped picking on each other after that and were good together for the last few days of my father's life.

Later, on the phone, Mary told me that near the end, on the last day, my father looked upward and whispered, "Shirley." And then he glanced downward, at my mother and Mary, and said, "Bye bye."

"Are you going with Shirley?" Mary asked.

"I'm going to tell my daughter that she loves me," he replied.

His last words on earth.

All week long, my sister Janet tells me when I phone her, she had been wanting to send my father a small bouquet of flowers with a note that said "I love you." This is something Janet never said to our father in her life. She didn't do it, but just before he died, when she was on the phone with Mary, Janet said, "Tell Dad I love him."

Janet said she knows that everyone will interpret our father who maybe art in heaven's final words differently, but for her, they were meant for her.

I don't think they were meant for me.

I'm just hoping Shirley really *was* there to take him across the finish line.

Afterword

I return on another plane from another trip east, another death, another burial. My father has been laid to rest beside Shirley in a quiet cemetery on a hill. All of his daughters were present, and Joanie gave a touching eulogy. After the burial, the Women's Altar Society of St. Helen's Church put on a huge brunch—forty dishes—and mourners filled the church hall. A few of my father's colleagues from West Point even came, though he retired from there thirty years ago.

In two days, my sister Mary will leave the North Country, and my mother will spend the very first night of her life alone. I feel concern about this. She has just turned eighty-nine, after all. But when I ask her if she wants someone to stay with her for a few days, she says, adamantly, "No, this is just what I have to face." Her voice does not tremble.

I have made a trip to Shirley's house to bury the remains of my Shirley candle. With a short-handled shovel, left by my sister in her flower garden a year ago, I dug a shallow hole and dumped the red shards into the earth under a maple tree that took root and started to grow along the driveway not far from her bedroom window several years ago. A "volunteer," they call it.

On the morning I leave, I finally summon the courage to open the local newspaper to read my father's obituary. It is strange and humbling to see a long life, any life, reduced to a few column inches. His is the last obituary on the list, but for some reason my eyes wander upward and there I find the name of Shirley's giant, Bill Dwyer. Knowing he spent the majority of his strange life in the nursing home, too big to move, I feel a sense of intense awe. I had heard from Marcia that he had not passed on way back in January when he reported seeing Shirley, but in the commotion of my life, I had forgotten to follow up on him. Now, seeing his name and my father's in the same obituary column, I remember Marcia's e-mail of long ago, just before I started my *Month of Sundays,* and I imagine my sister waiting there, on the other side, to escort her father, John Kress, and her friend, Bill Dwyer, through the Pearly Gates into the next world, whatever it is.

I arrive back home, having missed the whole second week on my new job. On the plane, I listlessly open a folder with fifty-one ninth and tenth grade compositions in it, but I cannot bring myself to grade them. I close the folder, close my eyes, sleep deeply until the plane touches down in New Mexico. I collect the Dodge Colt Vista out of the long-term lot. It is after midnight, and the streets of Albuquerque are silent.

I let myself into my *casita,* where Julie Reichert has placed fresh flowers from her garden in a ceramic vase. She has also collected my mail and placed it on the kitchen table. I sort through bill after bill but then discover a letter from Marcia, whom I saw in the back row at my father's funeral. I flop on the couch, slit it open with a pencil, and read.

> Julie-
> A thought:
> I compare my faith-belief-knowledge of God—the Great Spirit, the Big One—with my mountains. On a clear day, the mountains can be seen forever, in all their glory and majesty—easy! (Sure, there is a God.) On a hazy day—well, you can only see the few up close, but you know the rest are there somewhere. (I think there's a God.) On a totally cloudy day, you can't see the mountains at all. (Where are you, God?) But you still know they're there. You just can't see them! If I am the person who *knows* the mountains (God) are there and I tell you that, but, because it is cloudy, you yourself can't see them, you have to trust me, trust that I am telling you the truth. They *are* there.
> There is a God.
> Marcia

I run a hot bath, the kind that turns my skin crimson and causes sweat to break out along my hairline. Sitting on the side of the tub, swishing bath oil through the water, I think of Shirley's best friend, Marcia, up in her lonely mountain cabin, looking at the mountains, and thinking, God. I like to imagine that picture.

And I like to think of Shirley's newest friend, Paul Timmons, showing up at my parents' house to restore balance and put them back in touch with their lost love in my poor old Dad's difficult final days. I like to think of all the churches I've been to, too, of the way my life has revolved around searching for the spirit ever since my sister died, of my nieces and nephews, sisters, parents, friends.

I put a Billie Holiday CD into the player that Jimmy and Lisa gave me for Christmas. Lately, I listen to Billie every night when I soak in the tub. I light candles and watch the shadows they cast on the bathroom tile. I sing along: "If that isn't love, it'll have to do, until the real thing comes along." Of course, Billie sings it infinitely better than I do, but I try.

The next morning, this morning, I get up at five. A half hour later, I am in the car, heading north to the reservation. Back to work. It is still dark when I close the driveway gates and ease off, down Bridge Boulevard past the True Vine, over the Rio Grande, onto I-25. I feel tired but peaceful. A golden glow begins to edge over the ridges of the east mountains just before I exit the highway to head west.

At a particular place on Route 44, I round a curve onto the Santa Ana Reservation, and the urban sprawl abruptly stops. The city, the suburbs, everything is simply gone. The desert stretches before me like a sea with dune-colored waves, and the red rocks of the Jemez are a bright gash in the distance. You can see a hundred miles, I think, and a thousand miles into the sky. I hit this place at the same moment the morning light does. I am the only car on the road, and I feel like a giant curtain has been raised, just for me.

It takes my breath away, this beauty.

I pull to the side of the road and get out of the car, like Shirley used to. I feel Shirley in me as I stand there. And that's when I notice that I'm singing. Billie Holiday. But I'm singing, "If this isn't God, it'll have to do, until the real thing comes along."